"The moment when your legs give up is the EXACT moment when your heart gives more."

Michael D'Aulerio

The BASIC Marathon Guide

A Beginner-Friendly Program to
Running Your First Marathon

By:

Michael D'Aulerio

Disclaimer

Table Of Contents

INTRODUCTION:

Get Out the Door

My very first race EVER was a marathon. Running your first marathon can seem like an impossible goal. But the truth is… it's not.

Yes, it's an enormous accomplishment, and it will change your life for the better. But the fact is ANYONE can run a marathon. It just takes the right amount of FOCUS. Remember – wherever your attention goes is where your energy flows. With the right amount of focus, you become absolutely clear on your running goal. And clarity is one of your greatest powers as a runner.

One reason so few of us ever run a marathon is because we never truly direct our focus in running one. We never concentrate our power of clarity and make running a marathon a concrete goal. We just dabble our way into running, never deciding to fully master longer distances.

Don't become a wandering generality; be a meaningful specific. You must make a CLEAR and precise decision to run your first marathon. Make it CRYSTAL CLEAR in your mind. See it, feel it, and be it. When you make it a real goal, you will naturally take the right steps towards achieving it.

That very well may be the reason you stumbled across this guide. You may have made it a goal already, and just so happened to find this book.

But whether you are 100% certain on running a marathon or just hinting at the idea, this is the guide to get you there.

This GUIDE is just that, a GUIDE for running your first marathon. Because the truth is that no one can tell you exactly how to run a marathon. Each and every one of us is motivated differently, and the fact is that no one can run those miles for you. YOU run those miles, and you alone.

However, what I will do is SIMPLIFY the process. After running over 100 marathon and ultramarathon distances, here's what I can tell you about the majority of marathon tips you'll find. Most information online is either too OVER-COMPLICATED or too vague to understand. So allow me to suggest a simplified approach to get you across the finish line.

First, I will explain what a marathon is and talk about who should run one. I will then provide an easy-to-follow, beginner-friendly marathon training program so you can start right away. And finally, I will provide 26.2 training tips and 26.2 racing tips to help you along your journey.

Sounds like some pretty useful information, right? And when it's all said and done… you will have a PLAN… a SIMPLIFIED plan for crossing the finish line of your first marathon. With this plan, you will not only morph into the marathon runner you have always wanted to become, but you will have changed your life story.

Remember – if you want to change your life, then you must change your story. And crossing the finish line of a marathon will do that to a person.

Real quick, before we begin, here's a word of advice: Do not tell your goal to ANYONE. Keep it to yourself. Telling someone will only neutralize your motivation and discourage you from taking action.

What do I mean, exactly? Well, when you tell someone your marathon goal, it INSTANTLY becomes discouraging. For example, let's say you tell a friend you are going to run your first marathon. Seems harmless, right?

But here's the problem – by telling your friend, they already start to think of you as a marathon runner. And since becoming a "marathon runner" is a significant part of the goal, you begin to feel that you have already achieved it. That's because you have reached the identity goal. This occurs on a subconscious level. By prematurely achieving your identity goal, your drive slips away. Lose enough of it, and you will find yourself not even starting, or quitting as soon as training gets tough.

Studies have shown that wanting to have a particular identity, like becoming a marathon runner, is a critical motivator in following through on your training. Believe it or not, running is much more mental than it is physical. You will begin to understand this concept more after running your first marathon. But don't worry: in this guide, I provide tips and tricks for both.

Know this: You must not only run past the limits of your body, but you must run past the limits of your mind.

When you think a thought for long enough, like not being able to run a marathon, that thought turns into a belief. So even though running a marathon is tough physically, the toughest part is the mental race. What's most challenging is breaking past those limited beliefs you have created unintentionally. But here's the good news – those beliefs work both ways. Meaning: you can create helpful beliefs too.

Do so by focusing on the thought of running a further distance. Soon that thought turns into a belief, and that belief gives you the power to begin training.

So, if you develop the thought that you CAN run a marathon, and have ABSOLUTE certainty in your abilities, then you WILL begin training. And if you follow this guide, and relentlessly move forward, you WILL run your first marathon. And when you believe in your abilities, you can run ANY distance, including the distance you once believed was impossible. And in this case... I'm referring to the marathon distance. But, again, there are tips in this guide to help with that.

So now that you have set the intention of running a marathon... and decided to keep it to yourself... and understand the power of

ABSOLUTE CERTAINTY, let's quickly discuss what a marathon is, just in case you are entirely new to running.

CHAPTER 1:

Marathon… What Is It?

Without getting too much in depth, let's briefly discuss what a marathon is, and where it came from. A marathon is a long-distance running event, 26.2 miles long. You will find that most marathons are run on roads. Some, however, take place on trails. Marathons are both large and small events, ranging from a big city marathon to a small race in a rural area. For the more popular marathons, you must qualify or enter into a lottery. But for the majority, you can simply register online and run.

Throughout the marathon, there are aid stations. An aid station is a place where volunteers hold out plastic cups filled with fluids. Each runner is assigned a race bib that pins to your shirt on race day. The bib will contain the runner's race number, name, and a chip to keep track of your time.

When signing up for a big city marathon, you may be asked your projected finishing time. Based on that time, you are then placed into a particular wave. When the gun goes off, each wave will start once the announcer tells you to begin. Breaking up the race into waves lets the fast runners go first. It also spreads out the course, because of the large number of runners participating.

There are many other helpful hints to know about race day. However, between the training tips and racing tips I provide in this guide, you will be well prepared.

So, you now may be thinking, "Where in the world did the marathon come from?" Well, the marathon is inspired by an old Greek legend. It's based on a messenger who ran from Marathon to Athens in 490 B.C. The distance he ran was approximately 25 miles. The point of his 25-mile run was to spread the news of a victory in battle. According to history, the messenger Pheidippides collapsed and died after reporting the news.

As time progressed, the event became standardized at 26.2 miles. It gained popularity and eventually became one of the original Olympic events in 1896. We still run marathons to this day, and they have only become more popular.

That's the brief history. There are other specifics I did not mention. But this guide is not about the history of the marathon. It's about the future...

...it's about YOUR future. Your future as a marathon runner and your future as someone who can reach a goal they once considered impossible. So although anyone can EVENTUALLY run a marathon, we can't all just walk out the door right now and do it. We must first build our foundation. We need to develop a sufficient aerobic base. No one wants their house built on a shaky foundation. Is your foundation sturdy enough for marathon training?

Let's find out.

Next, let's discuss how much experience you should have BEFORE you begin to train.

CHAPTER 2:

Go the Distance

My greatest fear is you will read this guide and NOT take action. Remember – knowing is not enough, you MUST take action to reach your goals. And that's why I put EVERYTHING I have into these guides I write. I do so because I KNOW a percentage of you WILL take action. And it's in your DECISION to take action where your dream of running that first marathon comes true.

Every single one of your goals starts with a decision… a decision to try… a decision to take action. But you must take a NEW action, like following this guide.

What could be holding you back from taking action? Well, one of the most significant limitations that hold us back in starting a marathon training program is the question: "Am I Ready"?

Well, guess what? The answer lies within the question. Simply switch the order of the first two words and read it again…"I AM READY!"

Okay, so changing two words around doesn't exactly make you a marathon runner. But the same concept applies. All it takes is a few small adjustments in your training and, yes, you WILL be ready.

So who can run a marathon? The answer: ANYONE. As I mentioned, the first race I EVER ran was a marathon. Chances are, if you are reading this guide, then you have what it takes to reach the finish line.

However, it does come down to the particular individual and how well they can handle new stresses. Breaking past limited beliefs is difficult because we are attached to our beliefs. Proving our beliefs are wrong may make some people feel as if THEY are wrong. And, well, not everyone handles being "wrong" all that well. It makes them feel like a failure.

But know this: there is no such thing as failure, there is only results. Sure, sometimes you do not achieve desirable results, but coming up short is the best learning opportunity there is. So get the concept of failure out of your head. Remember – if you are in your head, you are dead.

Long distance running is not just a physical challenge, but it's a mental conquest. BELIEVING you can run a marathon is more than half the battle. But for some, they may want a half marathon under their belt first. While others may have the mental strength to jump into a training program with little experience at all.

For me, the marathon was the first race I ever ran. I started training for my first marathon when I was able to run seven miles. After that, training for a marathon was a mixture of the hunger to achieve it, and the confidence to believe it.

So, if you've run a 10-miler or half marathon, then you have plenty of experience to give your first marathon a go. And even if you've just run seven or so miles on your own time, then you know you can still do it.

But don't EVER count yourself out and think you are not qualified. Remember – ANYONE can become a marathon runner.

You were born to run. In life you sit, you stand, you walk, and yes… you run. There's nothing complicated about the process. It's just some of us put running on a pedestal like you have to be part of some exclusive club, and then forget that running is simply a part of life.

Between the gear, fuel, shoes, and everything else sold in the industry, running can sometimes lose its simplicity. So try not to make running a marathon more complicated than it really is. All you need is a pair of legs and the determination in your heart.

And if you are still reading, you definitely have the determination required. So are you ready to run ANY distance? Are you ready to run further? Are you ready to run your first marathon?

If so, let's jump into your beginner-friendly marathon training program.

CHAPTER 3:

The BASIC Program

When running your first marathon, have ONE goal and ONE goal only: cross the finish line. I will repeat this goal a few times throughout this guide.

I know: for most, running is about faster times and quicker paces. But when running your first marathon, this has the potential to backfire... and it usually does. You then learn a VERY HARD lesson about pacing and preserving your energy for the later stages of your race. Trust me, I know, I've been there. And unfortunately, although most push through this unneeded increase in difficulty... here is where some will give up.

But know this: finishing a marathon a half an hour faster or slower will not make you feel any less of a marathon runner. No, not at all. You are not going to think, "I only ran a four-hour marathon! I can't believe it! I'm so disappointed in myself!" No way! You are going to join the .5% club and say, "Woohoo, I am a marathon runner!"

As cliché as it may sound... remember, it's a marathon, not a sprint. So take your race easy, and your training even easier. Once you cross the finish, you will have enormous confidence in your running. That is where you can start speed training and running faster paces.

But first things first, let's become a marathon runner. Let's start by following the training program on the next page and taking it slow.

THE BASIC MARATHON TRAINING PROGRAM							
WEEK	MON	TUE	WED	THU	FRI	SAT	SUN
1	REST	3	REST	3	REST	REST	5
2	REST	3	REST	3	REST	REST	6
3	REST	3	REST	3	REST	REST	7
4	REST	3	REST	3	REST	REST	5
5	REST	3	REST	4	REST	REST	8
6	REST	3	REST	4	REST	REST	9
7	REST	3	REST	4	REST	REST	10
8	REST	4	REST	4	REST	REST	8
9	REST	4	REST	5	REST	REST	11
10	REST	4	REST	5	REST	REST	13
11	REST	4	REST	5	REST	REST	12
12	REST	4	REST	5	REST	REST	16
13	REST	5	REST	6	REST	REST	12
14	REST	5	REST	5	REST	REST	18
15	REST	5	REST	6	REST	REST	11
16	REST	4	REST	3	REST	REST	7
17	REST	3	REST	2	REST	REST	5
18	REST	REST	REST	REST	REST	REST	26.2

*Please note, in week 18, I recommend to REST the ENTIRE week. I may be the only running coach to recommend this. However, I've used this method for the majority of my races. Why do I recommend to REST the last week? Well, science proves that our endurance does not begin to diminish for 10-14 days. So a complete seven days of rest will allow extra time for your body to heal without losing any stamina.

It's important to recognize that your body experiences high levels of stress during a marathon training program. A full week off will help in the healing process, so you are ready to run, fully recovered, and completely recharged.

However, if you would rather run the last week, simply make week 17 your last week of the program. For example, instead of running six miles on Sunday, now Sunday will be race day. Meaning that week 17 will be your race week.

Also, you will notice the plan is built on running three days per week. Run any more, especially as a newbie, and you risk the chance of burn out or injury. Remember – you are training your body to BECOME a marathon runner body. You are not training for a marathon WITH a marathon runner body. When training for your first marathon, your body is not built yet for marathon running. So running fewer days, like three days per week, will bring you closer to achieving the greatest maximum results in the shortest period of time.

Running long distance is a JOURNEY. During this journey, you learn what works for you, and what does not. But as long as you take it slow, and allow your body time to recover, then problems are mostly all solvable before they escalate.

For example, when I began increasing my mileage for the first time, I was using a particular shoe. For five-mile runs, the shoes felt great. They were soft, supportive, comfortable, stable, roomy, everything you could hope for in your first pair of marathon shoes. But as I began running over 10 miles, I noticed my knees hurt and my shoes rubbed the back of my Achilles. The constant rubbing caused cuts and blisters.

But since I was not overtraining, I had time to solve the issue before it created an injury and ended my training early. What did I do to solve it? I went to a local running store and got fitted for a new pair of shoes. The new pair meshed well with my stance, step, and stride, and the knee pain and Achilles rubbing went away.

If I had been running five to six days per week, there's no doubt in my mind I would have injured my knees. That's why 65%-85% of runners injure themselves each year. It's not from running a longer distance. It's from overtraining and allowing small issues with their shoes or form to escalate into BIG problems. The type of problems that force runners to stop training.

So, with that, let's get into the training tips for running a marathon.

CHAPTER 4:

26.2 Training Tips

So now that you have your beginner-friendly training program, it's time to begin training. Before you get moving, take a look at the following 26.2 marathon training tips. They will help your training go a whole lot smoother. Use each tip to assure you get through your training and to the starting line of your first ever full marathon.

Let's get to training!

Training Tip #1: Have One Goal and One Goal ONLY

Setting your running goal is the first step toward turning your dreams into reality. I mentioned this tip earlier, but it's so important that it's worth repeating. And for those who like to skim read, you may have missed it the first time.

Before you begin, you need to establish your race day goal. This will help guide you through training with more efficiency. When you know EXACTLY what your goal is, you increase the odds of completing your training program.

I know: when you first decide to run a marathon, you want to run fast and get the best time you can. But allow me to suggest a different technique. It's a MUCH simpler one. On race day, have ONE goal and

ONE goal only: cross the finish line. And make sure your training reflects that. Once you get across the finish line, you will develop this incredible, unbreakable self-confidence. That is when you can start training for a faster time and at a quicker pace. Save the speed training for your second marathon.

Burnout comes easy when training for your first marathon. If you try to run super fast on every run, you have the potential to burn out quickly. Plus, on race day, focusing too much on speed can burn up your energy WAY too quickly. It's a cold and lonely place to be on 16 miles during your first marathon, out of energy, with 10 miles to go. Trust me… I've been there.

So, remind yourself that no matter what time you finish, you will still become a marathon runner. That's not just a goal you achieve, that's a goal you become, and it's yours FOREVER. During training, just focus on covering the mileage and feeling good while running. By putting one foot in front of the other, then one way or another, you WILL cross the finish line.

Training Tip #2: Get Fitted for Shoes at Your Local Running Store

Preparation is the key to a successful race day experience. If you haven't already, then before you begin training, go to your local running store and get fitted for a pair of running shoes. The store will determine the BEST shoe for your stance, step, and stride. A well-fitted pair of running shoes will prevent pain and injury. The same pain and injury that will force you to quit a marathon training program.

Believe it or not, most aches, pains, and injuries from marathon training stem back to your running shoe. It takes time for your body to adapt to new demands. If you are running with a shoe that throws your body alignment off, then the longer you run, the more pain you will feel. This could, unfortunately, lead to injury. For example, if you have flat feet and you are running in a neutral shoe, then I can almost guarantee you will experience knee pain. But fortunately, switching to a running shoe that supports over-pronation will eliminate the knee pain.

Sometimes, the solution you've been searching for has been right there in front of you all along, and you don't even know it. When I first started running, I had no idea shoes were designed this way. But when I started picking up my mileage, my knees and feet hurt more and more. Then, after getting fitted for a new shoe… POOF… the pain was gone.

Training Tip #3: Sign up for the Race and Choose a Backup

Whatever distance you give continuous focus to in your mind is the exact distance you will run in your life. With a specific goal, you will begin to attract the right circumstances to get you across the finish line. That's why I recommend you sign up for your marathon NOW… like right now. If you can, sign up for your race TODAY. There are many websites to find a marathon near you.

If you want to run a marathon, you must get to the island and burn your boats. So don't think… just MOVE. Also, it's not mandatory, but I recommend finding a backup race. No need to sign up for it, just find another marathon a month out from yours.

Why find a second marathon? The second marathon is your backup. You never know if something will come up, preventing you from reaching race day. If you do find a backup race, view its registration cut-off dates. Make sure there's time to register if you do in fact miss your marathon. That means your backup race should not be a big city marathon. These marathons tend to have early cut-offs and sell out fast.

Speaking of big city marathons, for your first race, DO NOT choose a lottery race. You need ABSOLUTE CERTAINTY that you are registered for the race. Save the bucket list races for another time. Only a few marathons require a lottery or qualification to get in. So you can still run a big city race for your first time if you wish. But don't worry, 99% of the time you will make it to marathon race day. So don't dwell on it.

However, if for some strange reason you do miss your race… what about training? How should you train for your backup marathon?

It's very simple. Just go back in your training plan to whatever week you are out from your marathon. Then continue training, and run your backup race. For example, let's say you caught a stomach bug the weekend of your race. And let's say your backup race is four weeks away and you are following the 18-week program from this guide. Simply register for that race and continue your training, starting from week 14 of the program.

Not bad, right? So you now know the importance of signing up for a race, and you know it's a good idea to find a backup. Now, you are ABSOLUTELY CERTAIN you will run your race, and NO EXCUSES will get in the way of your goal.

Training Tip #4: Upgrade Your Running Gear

There's no such thing as bad weather, only bad gear! Marathon training puts you outside on your feet for much longer than usual. Besides the basics like sweat-wicking shirts and shorts, here are a few items you may want to pick up…

Hydration Gear

Belts are the most popular form of hydration gear used on race day. If you decide to use a belt, then choose one to support your individual needs. Some belts hold bottles for fluid and others only a place to stash your gels.

I didn't use hydration gear when training for my first marathon. I just stuck a few gels in my pocket and went on my way. When I needed to hydrate, I ran into a store to grab a drink. On race day, I drank the water and sports drinks provided at the aid stations. The running shorts I wore had a zipper to make sure my gels did not fall out.

Rain Gear

Make sure you own a quality rain jacket. If you are running in the colder months, then buy one with insulation. The gear you run with can provide enough support to the point where you are completely comfortable in the rain. Remember – there's no such thing as bad weather, only bad gear.

Sun Gear

Protect yourself from the sun with gear like hats, glasses, and even cooling bandannas. And don't forget to apply sunblock! Also, if you're prone to burning then make sure you wear a shirt with sleeves. Your body needs a lot of energy to run, and sun gear will reduce the amount of energy utilized for cooling your body.

Compression Gear

If you haven't started using compression gear yet, I HIGHLY recommend that you do. It can surely be the difference between a good run and a bad run. Compression gear not only helps with blood flow, but it wicks away sweat and most importantly… it prevents chafing!

The most popular forms of compression gear are shirts, shorts, long sleeves, tights, socks, and calf sleeves. So find what works best for you. When I run, compression shorts are a must. I wear them under all of my race shorts. If there is a lining in my shorts, I cut it out with a pair of scissors.

Here's the best part: if you add an anti-chafing product and wear a compression shirt and shorts, you can completely eliminate chafing. That means no bloody nipples and no painful rubbing under the arms or down your pants.

GPS Watch

A GPS watch is almost as popular as running shoes when running long distance. The primary function of a GPS watch is to track your location when running. It tracks your distance, pace, and some will even track elevation gain. You can imagine how this information comes in handy during training.

The data allows you to monitor your distance when you train and maintain your pace when you race. But know that not all GPS watches are created equal. If you decide to make this investment, be sure it's with a reputable company. Once you find a potential watch, read its user reviews. Each review will provide experiences from other runners who use the same watch. This type of information is priceless when determining how the watch actually performs when you run.

The longer you run, the more necessary running gear becomes. When you reach a marathon distance, running gear will only help your experience on the big day.

Training Tip #5: Ease Into Your Training

No matter how slow you run, you are still ahead of everyone who isn't trying.

Now that you have a training program and a new pair of shoes, you are probably super excited to get started. And although I commend you for your enthusiasm, it's essential to control that energy. EASE into your training SLOWLY. If you jump out the gate to fast with too much effort, your body will pay the price. Your body is not ready for that amount of stress that soon. Your bones, muscles, ligaments, tendons, heart, and lungs all need time to strengthen. So does your MIND.

Our bodies break down, adapt, and grow. It's a progressive process, and it takes time. If you go too hard too soon, you could find yourself in trouble. Not only will you become incredibly sore, but you significantly increase your chance of injury. This combination has the potential to prevent you from moving forward in your training.

The key to endurance is patience. Our bodies need time to rebuild and grow. So work hard, run smart, and be patient. You may feel full of extra energy, especially as a beginner, but be prudent and take your time. Distance will come over time, but if you rush, injuries will come in no time at all.

Pace yourself. Remember – we are training for distance, not speed. Running too fast creates a lactic acid buildup and causes heavy breathing. Eventually, we tire out, and our muscles become fatigued. When we run long distances, we are performing aerobic activity. Aerobic literally means 'with oxygen.' It's when you're not breathing too heavily, you can hold a conversation, and are primarily burning fat as fuel. When you train, especially in the beginning, just take it slow and keep the pace steady.

So take your time, run your first few weeks at a very slow pace, and allow your body to adapt to its new stresses. Your legs will be grateful you did.

Training Tip #6: Warm up and Cool Down With EVERY Run

Before every training run, it's a good idea to walk for five minutes. Start to walk slowly; bring it to a fast walk, and ultimately transfer into a very slow jog. This benefits you as it warms up your muscles to prevent injuries. I never stretch before a run and do not recommend it. Your muscles are cold, and it will only result in injury.

After each run, be sure to cool down also. This helps to bring your heart rate back down and flushes out any lactic acid buildup in your body.

Here's an extremely helpful tip: After your training run, walk backward for five minutes.

After a run, walking backward helps. You are cooling your body down but using muscles and movements that you rarely use. Also, walking backward puts less strain on your knee joints and helps with lower back pain. A well-deserved relief for your overworked body.

Training Tip #7: Strive for Consistency, Not Perfection

Don't strive to be perfect, just be your version of an excellent effort. Striving for perfection when marathon training will often lead to poor results.

What do I mean exactly? Well, running every single training run on each assigned day for the entire length of your training program may not happen. We often live busy lives, so we must be open to change as we go.

Stay committed to your running goals, but flexible in your training approach. For example, *The Basic Marathon Training Program* above has you running every week on Tuesday, Thursday, and Sunday. But that doesn't mean those days are a MUST. It won't hurt your training if one week you swap your Tuesday for a Wednesday and your Thursday for a Friday. There's no difference if you run each week Monday, Wednesday, Saturday instead.

There's an old saying that a tree that is unbending is easily broken. So don't let an obsession for perfection compromise the goals you wish to achieve. Meaning, don't let perfection get in the way of your results; the results needed to run your first marathon.

And although running every single assigned day will be most beneficial, the truth is, missing a training run will NOT be a deal breaker. What's more harmful than missing a training run is holding yourself to an all-or-nothing training mentality. Life happens, and no one is perfect. If you strive for absolute perfection and miss a training run, then you will most likely quit your training program.

But if you are open to changes in your plan, and stay flexible, you can keep progressing forward, no matter what, and still make it to race day.

Training Tip #8: Make Unusual Hours to Train YOUR Usual Hours to Train

When we first start marathon training, for most people, we struggle with finding time to train. But if you keep looking for time in the same places, you will never find more time. That's because if you train the same way you've always trained, you will reach the distances you've always reached.

Here's the truth: if you are FULLY committed to running your first marathon, then you WILL run your first marathon. And time will never be an obstacle. There is ALWAYS time to train. 8:00pm to 8:00am is enough time to reach ALL your running goals. Now that I run ultramarathons, there are times I wake up at 1:00am and start running by 2:00am. I do this so I can run 31 miles before the start of my day.

To help, get to bed early and set your alarm based on 90-minute sleep cycles. When you do this, you wake up feeling refreshed and well-rested even with three hours of sleep. To make up for it, go to bed a bit earlier the following day. If not, just keep on keeping on.

Training Tip #9: Follow Four Steps to Master Your Fueling Technique

This four-step strategy will help you determine the best way to fuel during your marathon training program. Afterward, you will have a fueling strategy ready for race day. If you're new to running, then fueling may be confusing at best. With the vast amount of fueling products in the market and different techniques, it becomes unclear in which direction to head. And this is why I put together the following four steps on how to fuel.

Step 1: Determining What Fuel to Use

When attempting to master your race day fueling technique, you must first know what type of fuel to use. Seems easy, right? But new companies are popping up everywhere with new supplements flooding the market. I've learned a lot about fueling after going through the ranks to ultra distances. I've gone from gels and sports drinks to fueling all natural – no processed foods, no performance supplements, not even sports drinks. But I didn't always fuel so natural.

When I first started off, I fueled with the basics: water, sports drinks, and gels. And although I do not endorse an approach through supplementation, I DO recommend it for your first marathon. A gel and sports drink approach will keep things simple on race day. And a simple process is essential when you first start long distance running. Every great finish was once a simple beginning. What holds most importance is getting started, then you can fine-tune the details later.

23

The gel and sports drink approach works well for beginners to even the most elite marathon runners. But don't think this is the only way to fuel – you can try different foods or supplements. The key is to find a fuel approach that works best for you.

Step Two: Test how Your body Handles the Fuel

Once you choose the type of fuel you will use, the second step is to test how well your body will handle it. Different fuels can seem manageable when you consume them, but cause gastrointestinal (GI) issues when you run. GI issues are anything from nausea to abdominal pain to frequent bathroom use.

I'll never forget the time I had the bright idea to eat an entire box of fiber bars the night before a marathon. The race went from how fast I could get to the finish line to how fast I could get to the next port-a-potty.

The moral of the story is to stick with what you have tested, not what looks tasty.

Step Three: Determine Your Race Day Intake Level

Now that you have chosen your fuel and tested it, your third step is to determine your race day intake levels. There's a whole lot of data for how many grams of this and that your stomach can break down per this and that time. But if you ask me, as a new runner, the last thing you want to worry about on race day is counting calories. Plus, the data is based on averages, and every runner has different nutritional needs. Consumption cannot be standardized because one runner's intake will be different to the next.

The key to optimal performance is experimentation during training. Through trial and error and making fueling a practice, you will guide yourself to the best intake levels for you.

HERE'S A GREAT PLACE TO START: drink a 20oz bottle of your favorite sports drink 20-30 minutes before your training run. Then for the first 1/3 of your distance, drink only water, for the second 1/3 use sports drinks, and for the final 1/3 use a sports drink and gels. From here, you can tweak your fuel consumption to what works best for you.

Step Four: Practice Your New Fueling Technique on Your Long Run

The fourth and final step is to take your new-found fueling technique and practice it on your weekly long run. Bring your fuel in a hydration belt or stick it in your pocket. You can also bring your sports drink if it attaches to your belt. If all else fails, simply run into a store and buy what you need while running. Your run doesn't have to stop if you go into a store. There have been countless times I've run up and down the aisles of a grocery store to buy a drink on a hot day.

The fueling process can seem complicated, but it doesn't have to be. All you must do is pick a fuel, test the fuel, determine the intake, and practice it on your long run. By following this four-step process, you will quickly find a fueling approach that works best for you. From there you can tailor it and mold it into your effective race day fueling strategy.

Training Tip #10: Lube up in All Friction Spots

As a species, we've learned that friction creates fire – a discovery that changed the fate of mankind. But, when it comes to our bodies, not quite the discovery we want to feel in our running shorts! To prevent chafing, be sure to lube up in all friction spots. Also, many runners choose to wear compression shorts to assist with sweat absorption. The two combined are a powerful combination in the fight against chafing.

Personally, at one point while running 116 miles across the state of Florida, I ran with a handheld in one hand and a bottle of baby powder in the other – an ironically symbolic situation for an athletic running dad.

Training Tip #11: Run "One Straight Shot" for Long Runs

Running "one straight shot" is an extremely effective strategy for reaching new distances. When I was training for my first marathon, I used it on a few long runs.

Here's how it works…

1. First, take the total mileage of your training run and map that distance from your house. Try only to use one road, but you may need to use two to three major roads, depending on the length of your run.
2. Once you map the overall distance from your house, note the closest landmark. The landmark can be a cross street, restaurant, store, or something similar.
3. Next, have a friend, family member, or transportation service drop you off. Now it's "one straight shot" home, covering the entire distance of your training run.

For example, say you have a five-mile training run. Just simply get dropped off five miles from your house and run home. I've been dropped off as far as 40 miles from my house! Sometimes I left with no phone or money and hid drinks in bushes along the way. That way, there was no turning back, so running home and covering the distance was my only option.

Training Tip #12: Eat a Lot but Eat CLEAN

Most runners know that your fueling strategy has a direct impact on your running. But what about when you are NOT running? What are you putting in your body then? Yes, you can get through a marathon with a so-so eating regimen. But here's what I can tell you from experience: the better you eat, the better you feel when running. And isn't that the whole point of this running thing? To feel better? Better in our body? Better in our mind? Running, in addition to eating better, will accomplish both.

But what do I mean by "better" anyway? When I say "better", I'm referring to "cleaner." Eating more real food like vegetables, fruits, good fats, and whole grains, and less processed foods is vital. Eating clean by eliminating processed foods will allow your body to function the way it's designed. When your body metabolizes efficiently, more energy frees up for your training.

Ever run after eating a whole lot of junk? I have! It's never a pleasant experience. The performance we put out is a direct reflection of what we put in. Remember – you are what you eat. So if you put in a sticky bun, then guess what? You feel like a sticky bun! But if you put in super alkalized high energy veggie shake then BAM… that's how you feel.

Your body doesn't have the ability to turn poor nutritional choices into ones of high quality. Our cells, muscles, skin, and bones are built by the food that we supply it. We literally are what we eat. So eat clean, feel better, and you will run longer.

Training Tip #13: Nail Down Your Pre-Race Meal

As long as you eat clean, then eating one food over another will not make that big a difference. For example, eating a bowl of oatmeal with berries versus a banana with peanut butter will not make or break your run.

But here's what's important: find a pre-race meal that works for YOU, eat it during training, and use that EXACT pre-race meal on race day. Pretty simple, right? Eating a RELIABLE pre-race meal is much more crucial than calculating the "correct" portions of fruits to grains.

I recommend eating your pre-race meal two to three hours before running, and then have a 20 oz sports drink 20-30 minutes before running. The sports drink before your run provides quick convertible energy for your run and makes a HUGE difference in how energized you feel.

I currently do not use sports drinks and run on an empty stomach. But I DO NOT recommend this strategy in the beginning. Most likely, if you are just starting off, then your body is much more efficient at burning sugar than fat. So stick with the simple sugars, like sports drinks, and FIRST get through your marathon before experimenting with alternative fueling strategies.

Training Tip #14: Make a Repeat Song Playlist

Have you ever heard a song that you can't stop listening to? Every time it ends, you put it right back on? Has a song ever touched your soul so deeply that it makes you feel INVINCIBLE?

Whatever song gives you instant chills when hearing it, use it to your advantage. Make a playlist with the song and add it periodically three to four times in a row. For example, let's call it "Song A." Your playlist would look like this:

Song A, Song A, Song A, Song B, Song C, Song D, Song A, Song A, Song A, Song E, Song F, Song A, and so on….

This will make you feel ALIVE during training and inspire you to push through those long, more challenging runs. Music has the power to make you feel ELECTRIFIED when you run, helping you stay away from the lows of further distances.

Training Tip #15: Learn How to Make Hills Disappear

Hills always raise a lot of commotion in the marathon running world. That's because marathon races always throw a big one towards the half marathon and then another big one towards the end. But hills don't have to be a problem or something we dread. Our bodies adapt to the type of route we train on. So if you train on bigger hills, then running bigger hills will feel natural. And it doesn't require "hill training." Just simply run routes that are hilly… that's all.

I recommend running hills VERY slowly at first. Allow time for your body to adapt. Here's a tip I like to recommend…

Keeping your strides small and quick uphill changes the overall dynamic of a runner's motion. Try this – first, while walking uphill, take a few lunges. Next, make your way up the same hill but this time take small, shorter steps. Which takes less effort? It's the latter every time. Similar to shifting a bike to a lower gear, a short step requires more revolutions but less energy per revolution. In this way, the hills begin to DISAPPEAR, and your experience becomes much more enjoyable.

Training Tip #16: Use the Big Dominos of Good Running Form

Proper form always comes to mind for beginners. When you learn new techniques, especially when training for your first marathon, it's easy to get lost in the details. Instead of giving each new technique the attention it needs, we try to take on many different forms at once. Unfortunately, this only leads to confusion and poor form. We end up running awkwardly and forcing our stride, thus leading to pain and overuse injury. The development of an injury due to overuse is the number one reason runners stop training. It's the constant knee pain or foot pain developed from not taking the time to develop your footwork.

So how do you develop good form? Take one technique at a time, learn it, practice it, master it, then move on to the next. Make sure you work on each technique to the point where it feels natural. Also, first learn techniques that help the most. Master the "big dominos" up front that will have the most impact.

Keep reading, as I provide the big dominoes of proper running form. I have chosen three of the most beneficial techniques to learn first. With these three tips, plus a well-fitted shoe, you will run with much less effort and prevent common injuries in your marathon training.

1 – Forward Lean

Have you ever stood back and thought what running is exactly? Running is controlled falling. When you run, you are affected by one of the largest forces on earth: gravity. So instead of working against gravity, allow gravity to work for you. When you lean forward, you fall forward, using gravity for your propulsion instead of your legs. This allows you to run longer distances with far less effort. Also, leaning forward keeps your body in alignment. An aligned body will naturally put your feet underneath you while running.

2 – Mid-foot Strike

Now since your forward lean places your feet underneath you, it's much easier to practice a mid-foot strike. Landing mid-foot is the second-most useful technique to learn. A mid-foot strike keeps your body in alignment, which will help decrease the odds of injury. When performing a mid-foot strike, pay close attention to where your feet land. Make sure they land underneath or slightly behind you, as well as stay in line with your hips and shoulders. When you land mid-foot, you prevent yourself from heel striking. The heel strike stride contributes to many injuries runners face each year.

3 – Relax

When running long distance, like the marathon, your movement shouldn't be forced. You want it to be efficient and effective, yet relaxed and smooth. Don't force your stride. You're not "pushing down" when running, you're "lifting up."

New runners tend to tighten up and force their run, but running is the most natural form of movement there is. Forcing your run leads to stiffness and tension which wastes energy and decreases efficiency. So stand tall, bend your knees and elbows, take shorter steps, and relax into your run.

You shouldn't focus on all three techniques at once. Remember – the key is to work on one, master it, then move on to the next. A forward lean, mid-foot strike, and relaxing will alone have a tremendous impact on your running. This will decrease injury, increase efficiency, and make running much more enjoyable. These three techniques will be your foundation for proper form.

When you master these three techniques, your running will never be the same. Your first marathon will now come much easier with far less effort than before.

Training Tip #17: Prevent Soreness With Recovery

Most runners tend to put so much effort into their running that they tend to neglect recovery. But know this: we don't grow during the act of running, we grow during recovery. Our bodies stress, heal, and grow. So we need to run, rest, and progress.

But if we run-run-run then we stress-stress-stress. This provides little room to heal and grow. We break down during our run, but leave no time to grow back stronger. That's why, when new runners try to run five to six days per week, they tend to give up on their training program.

The simple fact is beginners need even more time to heal from running longer mileage. The amount of effort you give to recovery should be at least equal to the amount of effort you give to training.

So, when you see "REST" on your marathon training schedule, make sure you actually REST. During these days, you can take ice baths, go for walks, and even do some light cross-training. If you are okay with taking medicine, then you may want to use ibuprofen. If you do cross-train, I recommend not performing any intense workouts. But at the same time, don't laze around and do nothing. Movement increases blood flow, thus promoting a faster recovery. So even if it's only walking to the store, or standing at work, or making an intention to move every part of your body through the day, some movement is better than NO movement at all.

Using a foam roller is one of the best tools for recovery. If I could recommend only one type of exercise for recovery, it would be the foam roller. It loosens off the leg muscles and helps relieve tension and tightness in your legs. If you are new to the foam roller, it will most likely be extremely painful because the tissue is still very tender. But if you stick through the pain, it will eventually feel much better.

Remember this: the pain you feel on the roller today will eventually be the relief you feel tomorrow. For me, rolling at night is eventful. It typically consists of my two sons jumping on top of me for a ride, while trying not to run over my eight-pound dog in the process.

And make sure you get SLEEP during the week. Your sleep cycle is your healing cycle. So try not to neglect it. Sleep, clean eating, and healing-oriented exercise is the key to your recovery. And the reciprocal will be a more comfortable training run.

Think of recovery as the PREPARATION for your next run. Simply put, if you DON'T focus on recovery, then your run will be HARDER. But if you DO focus on recovery, then your run will be EASIER.

Training Tip #18: Cross Train, but Be Careful

Cross training between training runs can definitely help increase your aerobic condition. But here's my recommendation: NOTHING HEAVY ON THE LEGS. I say this because the blood flow for recovery is beneficial; however, you need to take advantage of your REST days. That is, give your body time to heal.

So what kind of cross-training is beneficial? Weight training your upper body, swimming, yoga, and even some light cycling. Just avoid heavy weighted exercises or intense fitness classes. Give your legs a break.

I would, however, recommend taking off one day from ALL exercise. The day I'm referring to is the one right before your weekend long run. For example, if you have a rest day on Friday and a 16-mile run on Saturday, take Friday off of ALL exercise. This will help your legs heal more and prepare them for pushing the limits and running longer.

So, cross-train, but take it easy.

Training Tip #19: Change Your Mind

Whatever distance you believe you can run is the exact distance you will end up running.

Did you know that at one time the four-minute mile was considered impossible? Experts even said your heart would explode! Fast forward in time, and now high school students can run a four-minute mile. Just wait until the two-hour marathon is broken – this impossible feat will soon become standard.

So how does this relate to marathon training? Well, marathons are not as "impossible" as you think. And no… your heart will not explode. Here are the facts: in the last ten years, there has been an increase of marathon finishers by 200,000 runners per year! Just like the four-minute mile, the more runners who do it, the more we believe just how possible running a marathon is.

Okay, so you may be thinking, "Well who says I'll actually finish on race day?" Don't worry, I have some numbers for you on finishing percentages as well.

The New York City Marathon currently has more than 50,000 finishers and at a finishing rate of over 98%! So, if you go through training, and make it to the race, chances of finishing are almost guaranteed. Why are they almost guaranteed? Because the atmosphere on race day is absolutely ELECTRIFYING! We feed off each other, the crowd, race day adrenaline, and the beautiful struggle that is marathon running.

You will soon realize that the hardest part of a marathon isn't the race at all. The most challenging part is the mental obstacles you face. Completing your training and destroying the limited beliefs that hold you back – that's when you become a marathon runner!

It's those runs when you're not racing for a medal or an online finish time. That's when you become a marathon runner!

It's those long days at work when you get home and go out for a run anyway. That's when you become a marathon runner!

It's when you sacrifice a night of good sleep so you can fit in a long run. That's when you become a marathon runner!

It's when someone says you're reaching too high, but you grab that shining star anyway. That's when you become a marathon runner!

It's when you fall down, pick yourself up, and say, "I STILL GOT THIS!" And most importantly, it's when you never EVER give up. When a runner makes a race look easy, remember this: people are rewarded in public for what they've practiced for years in private.

Ever hear of the famous Italian painter Michelangelo? Michelangelo is widely known as the most famous artist of the Italian Renaissance. He is the creator of the masterpiece on the ceiling of the Sistine Chapel. So what does painting have to do with running? Well, although you may think Michelangelo's artistry was a gifted natural talent, the truth is the guy worked hard. Michelangelo said, *"If people knew how hard I had to work to gain my mastery, it would not seem so wonderful at all."* It took an ENORMOUS amount of work to paint his masterpiece, and it will take an ENORMOUS commitment to your training to run a marathon.

But guess what? If you get through your training… the hard work is done. All you need to do now is walk to the starting line, wait for the gun to go off, and do what you do best… PAINT! Whoops… I mean RUN!

Training Tip #20: Your Body Never Lies…so Listen!

When you first begin to run, one of the first sayings you hear is "no pain no gain." Sure, I get the point – when you push against resistance, you grow back stronger. But if you're new to running, it's difficult to distinguish the difference between GOOD pain (growth-related) and BAD pain (injury-related). If you experience pain when you run, chances are something is wrong. I've learned many hard lessons figuring this out for myself.

You may also call GOOD pain "pain from gain" and BAD pain "pain from strain." Yes, your body gets tired, and you wear out mentally, and you sometimes need to push through it, but overall, running should be an enjoyable experience. If it's not enjoyable, then it may be time to reevaluate your approach. That's why you need to listen carefully to your body and adjust when necessary. The more you listen to your body, the easier it becomes to understand the different pains.

Take leg pain, for example. When you run, your legs might become tired, but when you push through it, they eventually grow back stronger. That's GOOD pain (pain from gain), and we expand by demand, so if you push through the resistance, you will only benefit.

But what if a new pair of running shoes was causing the leg pain? What if you overpronate from flat feet but are wearing a neutral shoe? Now, the more you run, the more pain you experience. If you push through this BAD pain (pain from strain), it will lead to injury. And leg pain is only one example…but a critical one. By listening to your body, you'll understand the difference between GOOD pain and BAD pain and your endurance will progressively grow.

Listening to your body will help get you from where you are now to where you are headed – the finish line of your first marathon. So take your time, run in the present moment, and listen to your body. What it has to say will only help.

Training Tip #21: Wear High Cut Socks

This may be the only time you will ever see this marathon tip, like… EVER. The recommendation is to wear HIGH cut socks. Make sure your socks sit well above your shoe.

Why do I recommend this? Well, I can't tell you how many runners I see who get blisters or who cut the back of their Achilles from low socks. But still, they wear low cut ankle socks. Many times you see marathon runners with low cut socks who put bandages on their Achilles. This way, they can continue running without pain.

But all of this unnecessarily added resistance can be avoided by merely wearing high cut socks. The socks don't have to be anything special, just a sweat-wicking material that sits above the top of your shoe. I wear compression socks for long runs and a high cut pair of athletic socks for short runs. As long as they sit a few inches above my ankles, there's no rubbing.

The less unneeded resistance you create, the more energy you can put into the natural resistance of running.

Training Tip #22: Be Cautious What You Wear Outside of Training

We focus so much on what we wear while running that we don't even consider the effects that our normal everyday attire can have on it. You know those new shoes you bought for that upcoming event? They could be the death of your marathon training program, and you may not even know it.

I remember buying a new pair of shoes for the gym and to kick around in on the weekends. But after wearing them for a few days, they began to cause knee pain. I've seen this issue in non-runners and those new to exercise many times before. Every time I mention shoes are the cause, and they make a change, I can't explain how much relief they receive. But being a long distance runner, these thoughts come instinctively.

If we don't want to run in a shoe that hurts our body during running, why would we do so when we are not running? Your running shoes are only worn a few hours per week, but your normal shoes are worn the rest of the time. The simple fact is that wearing a pair of shoes that hurt your body outside of running leads to injury while running.

And be careful on what size heels you wear – no one wants to roll an ankle only a few weeks out from race day. You never know what can happen. I'll never forget the time I stuck a box cutter in the side of my knee only a month out from race day.

The point is, what we do outside of running has a direct effect of what we do while we run. So be cautious of what you wear outside of running, and avoid unnecessary pain and injury by doing so.

Training Tip #23: Every Morning, Absorb Inspiration

The moment you wake up EVERY morning is the BEST time to absorb a dose of inspiration. It sets the standard of your whole entire day, and when marathon training, you will need it.

Marathon training can get tough. The difficulties extend far beyond your run. Waking up sore and running anyway is challenging. Living a healthier lifestyle and getting off the junk food takes a strong will. Staying consistent when training, even when it feels like an impossible feat, can be discouraging.

So it's even more critical to set the standard of your day... EVERY DAY. Take the initiative and be proactive. This way, you don't let external circumstances create the day – YOU create your day, and YOU are the owner.

If you let your normal habits dictate your day, you may be in trouble. What kind of trouble am I referring to? Well, the brain is not designed to be uncomfortable... it's designed to SURVIVE. So naturally, during marathon training, you will try to talk yourself out of running. "Don't go for that run, you are sore, your body needs to rest," or "Running is bad for your knees, don't you want to walk when you're older?" or "You're not a marathon runner, you are going to quit anyway, why even waste your time?" We are all haunted by similar negative self-talk that prevents us from following through on our training program.

Marathon training is uncomfortable. BEING UNCOMFORTABLE is stress on the body. And our brains interpret STRESS as a threat to our survival. So, your negative self-talk is not unusual, it's actually apart of the process. But guess what? Being uncomfortable, going through stress, and overcoming this type of resistance is EXACTLY how we grow. Every time we step outside of our comfort zone, GROWTH is guaranteed.

Overcoming these mental obstacles is the most essential part of our training. They are precisely what you need to overcome to become a marathon runner. What do you think happens during a marathon? More of the excuses come to haunt you... "Don't start, you're not a marathon runner, who are you kidding?" or "16 miles was a good run, let's call it a day, there's no way you can run another 10 miles," or "You are cramping up, things are getting dangerous, you should quit and go somewhere where it's safe."

But by pushing through those excuses during training, you are preparing yourself for overcoming excuses on race day.

Like weights in a gym, stress, excuses, adversity... when you learn to overcome them, they are not problems, but GIFTS in your training to help you GROW. To grow into a better runner. And to GROW into a mental GIANT who can crush those 26.2 miles because they believe they can do it! Because just like life, marathon running is a beautiful struggle filled with opportunities to better ourselves. So get inspired!

Training Tip #24: Follow the Process of Potential

First, understand that your potential is LIMITLESS. You can achieve ANYTHING in life if you give it enough FOCUS.

POTENTIAL

If you put all your focus into running your first marathon, then guess what?... You will run your first marathon. Understanding this fact alone will cause you to take ACTION.

ACTION

Reading this right now is the start of taking action. But that's not where the magic happens. Your dreams become a reality by taking your first step. The first step is when an impossibility becomes possible. So get dressed, walk out your door, and take action NOW. Remember – you can have unlimited potential, but if you do not take action then your potential stays just that... potential. Your dreams shrivel up and die in your mind. So, know your potential and TAKE ACTION.

RESULTS

The amount of action you take will have a direct effect on the RESULTS you receive. If you begin this marathon training program and give up, or take too much time off because you are sore, then you may NOT see the results of crossing the finish line. If you tell other people your training problems and let their comfort prevent you from moving forward, you may NEVER see the results of ANY running goal. You can do this. Don't let the opinions of others drown out your inner voice. The voice that told you to read this book – that's your best counselor.

But it will take persistence. You must take action each and every day. Understand that ACTION is the key that opens the door to your results. By understanding there is no such thing as failure, there are only results, then YOU WILL cross the finish line of your first marathon.

What's the secret to never giving up? Always try ONE more time. Crossing the finish line is a direct reflection of the actions you take every single day of your training.

BELIEF

And when you start seeing results, like progressing and running further each week, your BELIEF will be reinforced. You will start believing more and more what you are truly capable of as a runner: ANY DISTANCE. Soon, you begin to fall into an incredibly productive loop where the better the results you see, the more you believe in yourself, and the further you run. Endurance is a perpetual motion, as long as your heart beats. So know your POTENTIAL, take ACTION, acknowledge your RESULTS, and the more you BELIEVE in yourself, the further you will run. And in this example, far enough to cross the finish line of your FIRST marathon.

Training Tip #25: Change Your Words to Run Further

Through progressive training, your body can run ANY distance, but it's your mind you have to convince. And surprisingly, the words you use on a daily basis have a MASSIVE impact on the outcomes of your goal.

It's NOT "If I run a marathon," it's "When I run a marathon."

It's NOT "I want to become a marathon runner," it's "I AM a marathon runner."

It's NOT "I have not run a marathon," it's "I have not run a marathon YET."

The point: make sure to gut check your habitual vocabulary. What words are you using from day to day? Are you using negative words like *horrible*, *awful*, and *stressful*? Or are you using positive words like *astonishing*, *incredible*, and *spectacular*?

Does your training make you feel horrible? Or is the resistance of your training program morphing you into an incredible endurance athlete? The choice is there – it's ALWAYS there… the choice is yours.

If you change the daily words you use to describe EMOTIONS, you will INSTANTLY change the way you feel, how you think, and how quickly you become a marathon runner. Remember – language shapes our behavior and each word is an extra step in a positive direction. And in marathon running... you sure take a whole lot of steps!

Training Tip #26: Run One Day at a Time

When you train for a marathon, it will be overwhelming at times. Reasons to quit are always available, but guess what? So are reasons to FINISH. To help minimize the overwhelmedness of training for your first marathon, try to break up your training one day at a time. In this way, the training program will be only as far ahead as the next day, nothing shorter and nothing longer.

By implementing this strategy, each small achievement will eventually grow into one GIANT success. Isn't this true for all of our dreams in life? What's most important is each small achievement – the small actions we take each day towards our goals.

So it's not about the 10 weeks you have left, it's the five miles you have to run TODAY. Focusing on marathon race day is a fantastic motivator, but the key is to use the future as a TOOL, not to LIVE in it. When running long distance, you will start understanding the POWER of the present moment. By running one day at a time, you will get through training much easier and race day will be here before you know it.

Training Tip #26.2: Don't Think, Just MOVE

Sometimes, the hard part isn't the mileage of your run. Sometimes, what's most challenging is the distance from your bed to the door. HESITATION is the graveyard that dwells within potential marathon runners. When you hesitate, your brain receives a direct signal that something is wrong. It instantly goes into SURVIVAL MODE, and you begin to talk yourself out of it. Hesitation wires "quitting" into your brain. Do it enough, and it becomes a habit. Now, you will have trouble reaching ANY of your goals, running goals included.

I've been there, and I understand how hesitation can hold you back from running your first marathon. But after running over 100 marathon and ultramarathon distances, I have realized you learn not to think, you just MOVE.

Recently, I mentioned to someone I had a 30-mile training run the next morning. Since the weather forecast didn't look too great, they asked, "What will you do if it rains?"

My reply… "I WILL RUN".

They asked, "What will you do if it downpours?"

My reply… "I WILL RUN."

They asked, "What if it thunders and lightnings? What will you do then?"

My reply… "I WILL RUN."

Killian Jornet, one of the greatest endurance athletes on the planet, said…

"The secret isn't in your legs, but in your strength of mind. You need to go for a run when it is raining, windy, and snowing, when lightning sets trees on fire as you pass them, when snowflakes or hailstones strike your legs and body in the storm and make you weep, and in order to keep running, you have to wipe away the tears to see the stones, walls, or sky."

Sooner or later, as an endurance athlete, you learn to eliminate hesitation. Training becomes so hard-wired into your brain that there is NO other option besides to… RUN. And eventually, you stop thinking and just MOVE!

Until then, in the moment of hesitation remind yourself that overcoming hesitation is part of the training. Just like a training run, you must push through it. Becoming a marathon runner is about overcoming both physical and mental obstacles. And guess what? Each time you overcome hesitation, the easier it gets. Just like running, you stress, adapt and grow from it.

To make things go a bit smoother – to help – practice jumping out of bed every morning the second your alarm goes off. Don't hit the snooze, don't lie there and think, just get up and MOVE. Sooner or later, taking immediate action will become hard-wired into your brain.

Also, put your running shoes right next to your bed. As soon as you wake up, throw them on, and get moving.

Being grateful will also help combat hesitation. Wake up and be grateful. Appreciate your health, your strength, and the people in your life. Appreciate your drive, your determination, and your persistence for training. For life, for love, and for whatever else you can think of.

When you're in a state of pure gratification, you can only feel great, and that's the difference between getting out of bed to hesitate, or waking up to make your dreams come true.

Final Thoughts on Marathon Training

Remember – when you train for your first marathon, do not make it complicated. Keep the process simple. If you put one foot in front of the other, one way or another, you will make it to race day.

Once you get through training and race day approaches, you may wonder A LOT about marathon race day. Things can become overwhelming, but again… they don't have to be. So, read on as I provide 26.2 tips to help simply marathon race day.

CHAPTER 5:

26.2 Race Day Tips

So you've decided to take the plunge into the world of marathon running. Congratulations! Covering 26.2 miles on foot will not just change your athletic abilities, but it will also change your life.

Many highs and lows come with training and even more so on race day. But if these ups and downs are managed effectively, then the finish line becomes a near guarantee.

Under the assumption you're currently training, tapering, or finished with training, these tips will be your guide to a successful race day experience. These 26.2 running tips are designed to guide you through the course effectively and get you across the finish line of your first marathon in one piece.

A lot of energy can be wasted the morning of the marathon and even more so during the marathon. Your enthusiasm and energy can be a gift and a curse on race day. So be careful where you direct it.

Listen, you've made it to the starting line—you're here, you got to the island and burned your boats. Now it's time to stay focused; it's time to pace yourself, and it's time to develop a new understanding of what the word "POSSIBLE" truly means.

So without further ado, here are 26.2 tips to put you on a direct path through the entire 26.2 miles and over the finish line of a full marathon!

Race Day Tip #1: It's All About Location

First, visit the marathon website and read up on LOCATION. Be sure to find the answers to questions like, "Where is parking?" and "Where is the starting line?" If you're taking public transportation, then find the closest bus or subway station. If you're ridesharing then be cautious—the surrounding streets will be blocked off, so decide on the best drop off spot for race day morning.

Are you coming from out of town? Be sure to learn which hotels are recommended and exactly where they are located in relation to the start line. The last thing you want to do is walk two miles to the starting line then run an additional 26.2 miles. Only three more miles and you're an ultra runner!

Planning to drive to the starting line? Be sure to consider irregular traffic patterns. Your GPS might calculate 30 minutes the night prior, but drive the morning of the race with heavy traffic patterns, blocked-off streets, and closed down exits, and quickly watch 30 minutes jump to an hour or longer! Talk about a quick way to catch a case of the pre-race jitters. Remember, preparation is the key to an excellent race day performance.

Race Day Tip #2: The Race Expo Is Not Just for Bib Pickup Anymore

What is a race expo? Picture the entire running industry packed and condensed into one large convention center, filled with hundreds of vendors promoting everything from hydration gear to the cure-all for runners knee. That gives you a pretty good idea of what to expect. But, most importantly, it's where you pick up your bib, race tech shirt, and bag of race day sponsored goodies.

Underneath all the bells and whistles, the race expo is an excellent way to become familiar with the area, especially if you're coming from out of town. It's an excellent opportunity to check out the starting line area and verify the LOCATIONS you confirmed on the website.

Oh…and don't forget to pick up a few extra marathon t-shirts and a 26.2 magnet for your car bumper. When you complete the marathon, there's no harm in showing off a little. You definitely will have earned it!

Race Day Tip #3: Know Your Aid Stations

This one is critical. For most new marathon runners, it's crucial to know where each aid station is located. This could be the difference between hitting your time goal or hitting the wall. By knowing the mileage between each aid station, you can plan your fueling strategy accordingly. Make a plan on where to drink water, where to work in electrolytes, and where to take gels, blocks, or whatever other fuel you may use.

Race Day Tip #4: Hills Are Your Friend, Not Your Enemy

There's no escaping the hills. They are very patient. No matter how long you wait, they will always be there. So choose to embrace them.

Understanding the elevation gain of the marathon course serves two purposes. First, you will know what kind of elevation to train on. Already done training? Great! Reading up on the course's elevation will show the size of each hill and where they are located. Typically, you'll catch a relatively larger hill by the end of the half-marathon and one towards the end of the full marathon. Race directors like to keep the best for last.

Remember, it's not a sprint, it's a marathon, so pace yourself and use your energy wisely, especially uphill.

Race Day Tip #5: Keep Uphill Strides Small and Quick

While we are on the subject of hills here's a tip: keep your uphill strides small and quick. Think about it. If you put a pair of weights in your hands and walk uphill, what's easier? To lunge or take quick, short steps? Hills can be a great change of pace and a chance for different muscles to be activated. Hills can be your best friend or your worst enemy—the choice is yours.

Race Day Tip #6: If You Lose a Charge, You Will Lose Your Voice

Ever go on a run only to realize your watch is running low on batteries? Or for you music lovers like myself…there's nothing worse than being halfway through a run when your music player runs out of a charge. I remember one time I bought a new music player that stated the battery life was nine hours. It died in two! So I sang to myself for the remainder of the run. Sure, I didn't mind my singing, but I'm sure others did. My musical talents don't stretch too far beyond the morning shower. To prevent publicly displaying your musical arrangements on race day, be sure to bring a portable charger. This way you can grab a quick charge before the race or better yet, let me borrow it and avoid hearing my spectacular vocal variety!

Race Day Tip #7: Don't Stress Yourself to Sleep

Sleep the night before is not as critical as people make it out to be. The key is to get plenty of sleep the week building up to the marathon and especially two nights before.

Personally, I expect little sleep. Excitement and nervousness the night prior is just as common as drive and determination on race day. From my experience, lack of sleep does not affect race day performance if you make it a point to sleep well the week before.

It's funny…by not stressing the night before, you will likely end up with a few good hours anyway.

Race Day Tip #8: Change Your Mind to Change Your Running

When you first begin running, the marathon appears to be for the fast, tough, and strong. But although it takes much physical strength to get you there, the truth is, the mental strength will get you across that line before the physical ever will. Marathons are filled with runners of all different ages, different shapes, and different sizes. They push themselves, educate themselves, and most importantly, they believe in themselves and with that, anything is possible!

Race Day Tip #9: The Path to the Starting Line Is Through Your Excuses

We often fail before we ever begin. Most of the time, it's from focusing on fears we've created from thin air; for example, causes of failure or being unworthy. But what's incredible about becoming a runner is that it literally ONLY takes one step forward and poof—you're a runner.

We naturally develop excuses during training to stop us from even getting to the starting line. Discussing your excuses with someone else may only provide more comfort to quit before you even start. Your friends and loved ones mean well. Unfortunately, however, it's difficult to understand someone's motives to run a marathon unless you're a runner. I've learned to try and recognize excuses for what they are—excuses— and keep moving forward to race day. Because there's one thing I know for certain: if you look for excuses, you will always find them. Remember—there's no such thing as bad weather, only bad gear!

Race Day Tip #10: Choose Your Pre-Race Meal Wisely

Ask I mentioned earlier, I'll never forget the day of my third marathon. For some reason, I made the wise decision to eat an entire box of fiber bars before the race. I didn't get to see all the sights that day, but I sure saw all the porta potties. I finished, but learned a valuable lesson. Eat light and don't deviate from your pre-run training meals!

Race Day Tip #11: Master the Hidden Art of Bathroom Lines

Speaking of porta potties, be sure to arrive early for the bathroom lines. Sometimes you wait in line for 20-30 minutes. Excessively long bathroom lines are common in big city marathons. With 30,000 plus participants anxiously waiting for the gun to go off, using the bathroom becomes more of an art form than a form of excretion. Too early and you may need to go again, too late and the gun may go off midstream.

Also, as mentioned, roads and highway exits are typically shut down. Remember, unless it's a trail marathon, you'll be running through blocked-off roads and intersections. This will cause definite delays in the morning. So leave with time for unusual traffic patterns, alternate routing, and unexpected stalls like security lines. Better an hour too soon than a minute too late.

Race Day Tip #12: Follow Your Head-to-Toe Checklist

Personally, I run through the same mental checklist before every race. It's now become a pre-race ritual.

Here's what to do: once you are dressed, run through a list from head to toe to make sure you do not forget anything. Start with your head and work your way down to your toes: hat, check; headphones, check; compression shirt, check; you get the point. Write it down at first if it's easier. After a few races, it will just become routine. Either way, it only takes a few minutes and saves you from that gut-wrenching feeling during a race when you realize something significant was left behind.

Race Day Tip #13: Bring Extra Gear Today or Laugh at Yourself Tomorrow

This is when just-in-case packing comes in handy. Sometimes, you don't realize how cold or hot the day is until you're outside standing around. With extra gear, you can make any last minute wardrobe changes. Also, your gear may be broken and not noticed until race day morning. Trust me, you don't want to find out your hydration pack is broken, or your socks have a hole in them on race day morning with no backup. I've been there far too many times. Or here's a good one: you arrive at the marathon, not a cloud in the sky, and then, suddenly, you're struck by a severe downpour with no rain jacket. Yes, that was a "joyful" morning. Or the time I didn't realize my headphones were broken until I plugged them in. Or when I pulled my laces too tight, causing one side to rip off. Or when I was running a trail marathon, and the strap on my gaiter broke. The list goes on.

I only tell you these experiences to save you from the many race day stresses, and to laugh at myself, because…well, why not? The point is if you bring extra gear, you will reduce race day stress and focus on what's most important: running.

Where can you leave your bag? Marathons typically have a bag check-in station; however, I recommend you have a family member or friend with you. It's much easier to hand them the bag as you make your way to the start.

The point: bring extra gear and reduce unneeded stress.

Race Day Tip #14: Wear a Throw-Away

Layers can always be removed during a marathon. Depending on the weather, most runners wear a cheap long sleeve shirt and gloves to toss on the sidelines once their bodies warm up. If you're debating on whether to wear an extra shirt, just do it. If you overheat, take it off and throw it aside. The beginning of the course is filled with throw-away shirts and gloves. So make sure it's a shirt you don't mind losing. If it's a big city race, chances of seeing that shirt again are slim to none. If it's a shirt you can't part with, then meet a friend a few miles along the course for the hand-off.

Race Day Tip #15: Aid Stations Are Great Meetup Spots

Here's a good tip for marathon day: have a family member or friend meet you at the first aid station with your race day bag. Maybe you forgot to apply Vaseline or suntan lotion. Or maybe that winter hat suddenly seems like a good idea once you feel a cold breeze on the course. You may even forget something crucial like your fuel. Or maybe your hydration belt breaks once you begin. By meeting a family member or friend at the first aid station, you can get the problem fixed early on and keep your head in the race.

Race Day Tip #16: GPS Watch Battery Life Does Not Last Forever

I can't tell you the number of times I've witnessed runners stressed out about their GPS watch on race day morning. Most of the time, it has to do with little or no charge. If you absolutely need your GPS watch on race day, then be absolutely sure it's charged and works properly. If your watch does fail, here's the good news: most marathons have a time clock set up every mile or so. This makes it easy to keep an eye on your pace.

To calculate your pace on race day, just take the total distance you've run thus far and then divide it by your current running time. For example, if you reach the 10-mile marker and the clock reads 1:20:00, just divide 80 minutes by 10 miles, and your pace is eight minutes per mile.

If you forget the formula or like me, you prefer writing out equations to calculate…just ask someone. Most runners will have a watch on and know their pace, so if you're running next to them, then your pace is the same. Try to relax, take your time, and enjoy the race.

Race Day Tip #17: Lube Up for a Smooth Ride

Lube up all friction spots. You will thank yourself later in the race. Reapply during the race if needed and more so if it's raining. Compression gear can also help. A little chafing during a six-mile run will do no harm, but chafing at six miles with 20 miles to go will disrupt your pace and eventually become painful. So lube up and enjoy a smooth ride.

Race Day Tip #18: Be the Tortoise, Not the Hare

When the race begins, it's common to get a rush of adrenaline, and you may not even realize it. This causes a much quicker starting pace. If you give in to this, it will certainly catch up with you later in the race. I remind myself of this rush at every new starting line. Similar to the classic tale of the hare and the tortoise, it's important to keep a slow and steady pace. I stay in tune with my body and back my pace off slightly.

Personally, I do not wear watches. I run on feeling. From experience, I'm usually able to notice the difference between an adrenaline pace versus a race day groove.

During one of my first marathons, I noticed a super-excited guy running next to me. He was smiling, waving to all the bystanders, and jumping around for a number of miles. I remember thinking to myself, "I hope he's conserving some of that energy." Up by mile 16, I saw the same super-excited guy lying flat on his back on the side of the road. He was the hare, not the tortoise, and unfortunately, he dropped out.

Race Day Tip #19: Run Your Own Race

There are many runners of all different shapes, sizes, and speeds. Try not to get caught up in attempting to run faster than the person next to you. It's a long race, and this common mistake can cost you a high amount of energy too fast. It's a tough and lonely place to be out of energy on your 16th mile with 10 miles to go. Remember, the real race is against yourself. Let your internal control affect your external environment, not the other way around.

Race Day Tip #20: If You Experiment, You Could Forget Your Name

It's a good idea on race day to fuel the same way you've fueled during training. I seldom ever try something new on race day. I've learned the harm from this first hand. Race day is not the day for experimentation.

One race, before I started fueling all natural, I used whatever was handed out at the aid station. Between this, the heat, and hydration issues, I pushed myself to a point where my body control was lost, and I forgot who I was. I literally couldn't tell you my name or what I was doing. I finished, but it was dangerously difficult, and it took several days to get myself back to normal. This is a worst-case scenario, but the point is to be careful and stick to the plan.

Race Day Tip #21: Wear Your Same Old Fresh Shoes on Race Day

Stick with what works. Race in the same model shoe you trained in. Sure, a new model shoe may feel fine during shorter runs, even when you taper. But sometimes issues with a new shoe aren't unmasked until you run longer mileage. Plus, purchasing a new pair of running shoes with the pressure of race day around the corner is never a good idea. With as much uncertainty as you face during your first marathon, add some certainty, and wear a shoe you can absolutely rely on—the shoe you know best.

If your shoes have 150 miles or more on them, it may be time to pull out a fresh pair. The marathon will most likely be your longest run of the year, so the more cushion, the better. I typically rotate two or three pairs during training to prevent this issue. Also, sometimes bring out a new pair when it's time to taper. This keeps your shoes fresh for the marathon, but with just enough wear to mold well with your stride.

Race Day Tip #22: Have One Goal and One Goal Only

It's tempting to go after fast times and placements, but for your first marathon, I strongly recommend you avoid these temptations. I tell you from experience: make your one and only goal to finish. As you will notice, I recommend this tip for all distances. Once you have the first marathon under your belt, your aerobic base is built, and your confidence is high. Then go for a PR. By making your goal to finish, you will avoid energy-wasting behaviors and get yourself across the finish line in one piece.

Race Day Tip #23: A Mantra Will Lead You to the Peaks of Race Day

Create a strong and purpose-driven mantra or find a quote that sincerely moves you. When times get tough on the course—and trust me, times will get tough—start repeating that mantra in your mind, or say it out loud over and over again. This is a great way to pull you out from those race day lows.

Or better yet, add a song to your playlist that truly inspires you, you know, that song that gives you the chills every time you hear it. Once you've decided on the song, create a new playlist. Next, add the song 20 times. This way, when you slip into a low point of the race, that unavoidable valley, turn on the song and play it over and over again until your back upon a peak. Sing, if it helps! Running with high spirits can change your entire marathon race day experience.

Race Day Tip #24: See the Finish Line In Your Mind

Visualization is a powerful skill set to have. When you picture yourself crossing the finish line over and over again, it can have powerful effects. There's a system in your body called the "reticular activating system," which helps your brain decide exactly what it should be focusing on. For example, ever decide you want a particular car, then start seeing it everywhere you go? That's your RAS at work.

When you have a purpose and focus solely on achieving your goal with complete certainty, you will influence the RAS system, and you will begin to pay special attention to the things that will help you achieve it. And the process is easy. Visualize the finish line, see it, and watch it happen.

Race Day Tip #25: Schedule a Meeting for After the Race

I can't tell you how many times I've walked around aimlessly after the race searching for friends or family. After a marathon, especially a big city marathon, the majority of bystanders will be huddled around the finish line. The chances of your friends and family seeing you cross the finish line reduce as the crowd becomes larger. That's why it's essential to coordinate a time and place to meet after the race. Trust me—your legs will thank you for it.

Race Day Tip #26: Take In the Moment

This is your first marathon, so smile, and take it all in. Take in the sights, take in the sounds, and take in the experience. It's hard to believe it, but race day will be over before you know it.

The next morning comes fast, and soon enough you will be lying in bed with a sore pair of legs thinking back on your experience. So make the race consist of triumph and joy instead of pain and regret. Force the issue. You only run your first marathon one time, so make every minute count!

Race Day Tip #26.2: REMEMBER TO HAVE FUN!

Why do we go after our running goals in the first place? Simple; running makes us feel more alive. Progress is happiness and allows us to feel alive. It's our human nature.

That's why we hear endurance athletes say that there is beauty in struggle and there is magic in misery. In essence, stress is part of who we are; it's our way of life. When we struggle and push through the resistance, we feel alive! Through stress, we become closer in touch with who we are as human beings. Everyone wants to see the view from the top of the mountain, but all the happiness and growth occurs when you're climbing it. You will begin to understand this as you build your endurance. And by following The BASIC Program, building your endurance, you shall.

The most significant problem you'll face is fear. You fear that you will fail, you fear that you will give up, you fear that you won't finish. But fear is not only stopping you from reaching your running goals, but it's also preventing you from being yourself. Fear is stopping you from becoming who you are meant to be, a person who can run a marathon!

The key is to have fun when running a marathon! Have the guts to show up on race day. Have the guts to be terrified, or tired, and push through the pain anyway! In all the attempts of trying to prove something to yourself, remember that it's all for the reason to feel alive and become a better self. Never lose sight that running helps shape you into the person you want to be. And never lose sight that it should be FUN!

Final Thoughts on Marathon Race Day

Now you have *The BASIC Program*, as well as 26.2 tips for training, and 26.2 tips for reaching the finish line of your first full marathon. As you can see, if you stick to your training, and manage your race day experience, you can become a marathon runner in no time at all.

Lastly, flip the page and let's bring it home. In the conclusion of *The Basic Marathon Guide,* you will learn the ultimate benefit of this entire program.

CHAPTER 6:

26.2 Marathon Mindset Tips

Everyone has to start somewhere when training for a marathon... but where?

In traditional marathon training, you focus heavily on your physical stamina. You progress upwards from the 5k, to the 10k, and then the half-marathon. And if you are confident enough, you sign up for your first marathon. And there's nothing wrong with this approach. Yes, it can get the job done, and you have a training program in this book to do so. However, most will run into marathon-preventing issues along the way. That's because if you only focus on the physical, you're missing the most potent ingredient of all. You are missing the MENTAL side of training.

Building my mental strength is how I went from running a few miles on a treadmill to jumping right to my first marathon. Yes, I trained my body intensely, but I put a heavy emphasis on building my mental strength as well. By developing mental strength, or what I like to call a "marathon mindset," your mind will guide your body forward. Conversely, if you focus solely on physical training, you become vulnerable to mental blocks and limitations. Here's where most end up lost in the details of training, suffer from an injury, or burn themselves out. And maybe worst of all, they become COMFORTABLE at running shorter distances.

As a runner, COMFORT, similar to kryptonite for Superman, will block your abilities. It will prevent you from reaching a further distance. Comfort will prevent you from running a marathon. You must embrace the struggle and look beyond the pain. Start to see being uncomfortable as a signal of growth, not lack. The struggle is a part of the process. You must stress before you can grow. Just like the muscles of a bodybuilder, you expand by demand.

That's where developing your marathon mindset comes in. It helps you see marathon training from a new light. Running a marathon is not some impossible feat designed for elite runners. It's for runners like you who want to push the limits of everyday life. Because everything you could ever want, whether in running or life, patiently waits right outside your comfort zone. And if you keep moving forward and run a marathon, you experience something special. Something EXTRAORDINARY.

Running a marathon will not just provide an unwavering amount of physical fitness. But it will completely transform your mind. Crossing the finish line of a 26.2-mile race will reshape your life. Yes, it improves the obvious, like your endurance and power. But it also enhances the not-so-obvious, like your confidence and mental stamina.

I can tell you from experience. After running my first marathon, I went on to run more marathons. I then jumped into the ultramarathon world. I ran 50ks, 50 miles, 100ks, 100 miles, and even longer. I also ran a grueling 200-mile race. And guess what? I don't plan on stopping there.

But even after the many finish lines I've crossed, I'll never forget the final stretch of my first marathon. It was mind-blowing. The final stretch of my first marathon is where the magic happened. And you know what? It's where the magic will happen for YOU. I can still see it in my mind…

The marathon finish line was faintly visible in the distance. It didn't make sense at the time, how "someone like me" could finish a marathon. I even began developing self-sabotaging thoughts. And the same self-sabotaging thinking also affected my body. It was strange, but every step forward felt like two steps backward. I felt stuck inside a pit of marathon mental quicksand, and I was struggling to climb my way out. My brain could not comprehend what my eyes were witnessing. It began to short circuit! I could have sworn smoke was puffing out my ears!

Okay… maybe the smoke was a hallucination. Okay… the smoke was definitely a hallucination. But you get the point!

It was similar to a weak leg dream. You know, when you are being chased, but you can't pick up speed. No matter how much effort you give, you can't gain momentum. And every step makes your legs heavier than the last. That's precisely how the final stretch of my first marathon felt.

But if you dig deep enough within yourself, you will push through the resistance. Here is where you experience an incredible phenomenon. It's rather spectacular. You see, once your brain starts accepting the impossible is possible, the dynamics change entirely. Suddenly, the self-doubt relieves itself, and you SMASH through your limitations straight across the finish line. And once you make it to the other side, you experience a paradigm shift.

The finish line of your first marathon is like a metaphorical wormhole to a new dimension… to your new life. When you cross that line, you begin to understand the only barrier that held you back was your limiting beliefs. You begin to understand that the only barrier that EVER holds you back is your limiting beliefs. Because through adaptation, progressive training, and patience… ANYTHING is possible. Even running a marathon. And it all begins with your thoughts.

Never forget that the strength of your mind is beyond comprehension. Your thoughts are POWERFUL. Your thoughts shape your reality. Understand this: what you think on a regular basis magnifies in your subconscious. And if you hold onto a thought long enough in your conscious mind, it turns into a belief that enters your subconscious. Now it's a part of the blueprint that designs your life. It's what you perceive as your reality. Better put, thoughts are the cause, and circumstances are the effect. Your external world is a direct reflection of your internal world.

So, what's the problem with your thoughts turning into beliefs when it comes to marathon training? Well, there is no problem, if you can observe them. The key is to make your thoughts self-fulfilling instead of self-limiting. But unfortunately, most of our thoughts are naturally negative.

Here are some numbers that may shock you… Did you know that we have between 50,000–70,000 thoughts per day? I know, human beings do A LOT of thinking. So, don't worry… you're not alone.

And this level of excessive thinking wouldn't be a bad thing if we didn't naturally think so negatively. You see, for the average person, 80% of those 50,000-70,000 thoughts per day are NEGATIVE! I know, pretty scary… but wait, it gets worse…

Here's what's most alarming – 98% of our thoughts are recycled from the day prior! So not only are we unconsciously recycling our thoughts for years, but the majority of them are NEGATIVE!

70,000 thoughts x 80% negativity = 56,000 negative thoughts! No wonder 75% of the world's population reports to experience moderate to high levels of stress on a daily basis. We are not exactly setting ourselves up for success.

But you know what? I don't see 56,000 negative thoughts, I see 56,000 thoughts of opportunity. Do you see the possibilities? The opportunity? The potential? Think about what could happen if you flip a portion of those negative thoughts into positive ones. Consider how much YOU would change. Consider how much the WORLD would change.

After some thought, circle back and think about what your chances would be NOW at finishing a marathon. That's why running a marathon can be so hard for so many people. Not because it's difficult physically, although it will challenge your physical body. But the mental side, if not trained, will demolish most marathon goals before they even begin. Think about it. If every time you consider running a marathon you think, "I'm not a marathon runner," how could you ever begin? Or if during every training run you think, "I could never run 26.2 miles," how could you ever finish the program?

And if you hold those negative thoughts long enough, they begin to spin in your mind. Remember – 98% of our thoughts are recycled from the day before. If you don't start believing in yourself, good luck even putting on running shoes. You'll talk yourself out of it every time. If you stay in your head, you are dead.

In this way, you are adding more resistance to your marathon then is required. Compare it to the physical side, and it's like making the hills higher than needed. Or it's like racing your first marathon and running around the block 100 times before the start. Why add extra resistance? Isn't 26.2 miles enough for your first marathon? You wouldn't do it physically, so why do it mentally? Why make your mental hills the size of Mt. Everest when other runners are sprinting schoolyard hills? And if those negative thought loops remain unchanged for long enough, and they turn into limited beliefs, those beliefs eventually become concrete. And here's where people don't even consider running a marathon.

But don't worry. If you are reading this, then you are not there yet. And I'm going to help make sure you NEVER get there. So to develop a marathon mindset, we will start by pulling out the weeds and planting acorns that grow into oak trees. In other words, we will begin by eliminating your negative thoughts and replacing them with positive ones. Because here's the fact: if you think running a marathon is only for incredible athletes, then you are mistaken. ANYONE can run a marathon if they are hungry enough to succeed. I won't even bring up the man who is over 100 years old who runs marathons…

Okay, I just brought him up…Yes, it's true, and there are runners in their 70s crushing world records. The marathon is a distance, not a unicorn. Crossing the finish line is not some impossible feat, it's an outcome to a process you follow, and a mindset you develop. And here's the good news: if you are the one who created your limiting beliefs, then you are the one who can change them. All that's required is a directed awareness. When you see a negative belief, acknowledge it, and replace it with a positive one.

So wouldn't RIGHT NOW be a good time to start?

If you answered YES, then read below for 26.2 tips for developing a marathon mindset. You can use each tip to help you run your first marathon. Each piece of advice will help pull those negative thoughts you have towards running out of your subconscious. And over time, you will naturally begin to develop a marathon mindset. A mindset that will demolish limited beliefs and catapult you straight across the finish line.

Marathon Mindset Tip #1: Have Absolute Certainty in Your Abilities

Before you begin training, you must believe in your abilities. Have ABSOLUTE CERTAINTY that you can run a marathon. Certainty can be developed like a muscle, so practice using it in different aspects of your life. And when it comes to running a marathon, be ABSOLUTELY CERTAIN you will finish. Do not give yourself a way out.

Marathon Mindset Tip #2: You Are Human and Don't Forget It

Your mind is a muscle too. The metaphorical physical mountain of a marathon is a steep climb. But it's a rolling hill compared to the monstrous mountain in your mind. Fortunately, though, you're taking a chop at the monster's legs by reading this book.

Your mind is the most powerful tool you have. Change your mind, and you will change your life, starting with crossing the finish line of a marathon. So remind yourself on a daily basis that you are a human being. And perhaps the genius of the human animal is our adaptation response. By applying stress, we break down, heal, and grow back stronger so we can meet new demands. You are a human being. You stand, you walk you sit, and yes… you RUN.

Marathon Mindset Tip #3: Feel the Finish Line

Running a marathon is an extreme physical challenge. But the mental obstacles are even more taxing. If you understand that the marathon is both physical and mental, then you will be much better off. And that goes for both training and on race day.

Waking up two hours early to train… that takes mental strength. Walking out the door with a sore pair of legs… that takes mental strength. Tackling each training run week after week without giving up… that takes mental strength. Preparing for a marathon is a mental journey… but it's a journey worth taking. Know of this journey going in, and you will be well ahead of the rest. So, condition your mind by practicing mental imagery. I've already mentioned visualization, but to complement it, make sure to FEEL the emotion.

The brain doesn't know the difference between your thoughts and reality. So, hold an image in your mind of the finisher medal in your hands after crossing the finish line. FEEL the achievement. FEEL the excitement. FEEL the relief. Adding emotion to visualization is the secret ingredient to speeding up the process and assuring you follow through on your training.

Marathon Mindset Tip #4: Redefine What Failure Means

Understand what failure truly means. Although I don't like to use the term, "FAILURE" is not a word to tell you who you are. It's to inform you about a way that doesn't work. It's to educate you and to test you to see how bad you really want it. For example, don't see a missed training run as a failure, see it as a change in your plans. And be sure to take corrective action, so you don't miss one again. Or if you run under target pace, don't feel as if you failed during your run. Find out what mistakes you made and use them as a lesson to improve your next run. When you give failure this new meaning, you'll be willing to try just about anything, even a marathon.

Marathon Mindset Tip #5: Develop Helpful Habits

Hesitation has the potential to cripple your training. But once you get moving, you feel much better. How many times have you felt incredible in the middle of a run? Once your body warms up and is moving, your thoughts begin to change. Most of the time, you can't imagine why you didn't want to run in the first place. But the most challenging part is actually getting to that moment. That's why what's most challenging for some is not the actual run itself. What requires the most effort is dragging yourself out of bed and out the door.

If you repeat an action for 21 days in a row, it becomes a habit. So, for 21 days, jump out of bed the moment you wake up. No snooze but, no social media, no second thoughts. Just open your eyes and jump out of bed. After a while, you will feel pulled to wake up and run. It won't feel like you are pushing anymore.

Marathon Mindset Tip #6: Use Preparation to Combat Hesitation

Remember – hesitation is a mental obstacle. But when you develop a marathon mindset, hesitation is just a quick hurdle to overcome. To help, lay out all your running clothes the night before a training run. Put your running shoes right next to your bed. Fall asleep for a few hours, wake up extra early, and train. Then the following night, go to bed early if you want to catch up on sleep. I can't tell you how many times I've woken up at 3:00 am on the weekend or before work to run a 20-or-longer-mile run. So wake up, don't think, and get right out the door.

Marathon Mindset Tip #7: Meditate and Be Grateful

Staying on the same topic, another method to overcome hesitation is to practice gratitude. Make gratitude a daily ritual. I've mentioned gratitude earlier in the book, but it's so important I want to dig a bit deeper.

I mention gratitude a lot in my writing; I do so because it's one of the most powerful practices I know. When you are grateful, it's impossible to feel bad. And in a sport where being uncomfortable is a guarantee, gratitude will help you along the way.

In life, we can sometimes feel unfulfilled. You know, a feeling of emptiness. Well, that's where being grateful comes in. When you are grateful, then what you have is enough… who you are is enough… the world is enough. Do you see what happens? The empty hole begins to fill. When you focus on what you WANT, rather than what you HAVE, you feel like something is always lacking or empty. Similar to a hole. But when you are grateful for what you have, there is no hole, that is, you feel as if NOTHING is missing. Now you don't feel empty or unfulfilled.

If you practice gratitude on a regular basis, then your motivation to run will last a lifetime. Now wake up to train and tell me how you feel! To bring gratitude into your training, meditate before your run. Breath deep and focus on three things you are grateful for. Spend a few minutes on each one separately. Be grateful for the people in your life, your fingers and toes, health, love, nature – whatever brings you joy. Be grateful for how your heart beats all day every day without effort. That's enough to change your mood drastically. What a gift your heart is.

Sometimes it's tough to get going with appreciation and gratitude. But once you reach a grateful state, appreciation pours out like an untapped faucet. So it's essential to focus on something really close to your heart first. For example, to break out of the typical morning "what if" thoughts, I focus on my kids and their big bright smiles. I picture them laughing and saying "Daddy." From there… my gratitude flows in abundance.

Marathon Mindset Tip #8: Run in the Present Moment

Try to avoid over-complicating the process of running a marathon. Keep the process simple. If you put one foot in front of the other, one way or another, you will make it to race day. That's why I say that running can be so much more than moving your feet forward. Or it can be just that: moving your feet forward.

When you think about it, that's all running is, moving your feet forward. It's controlled falling. Running a marathon is simple. No, not easy, it's SIMPLE. There's not all that much to it. There is literally a clear paved path from beginning to end, and all you have to do is move your feet forward. Yes, there are challenges like fueling and chafing that you overcome and learn from. But even during your most significant moments of adversity, if you keep moving your feet forward, EVENTUALLY the finish line will come… it always does.

To help, practice running in the present moment. To do so, focus on your breathing and your five senses. Or keep running towards the next spot ten feet ahead. And when your mind drifts, observe your thoughts. Don't get lost in them. When you run in the present moment, the finish line vanishes, and time becomes an illusion. Now every mile is the same mile, and you can run any distance, including the marathon.

Marathon Mindset Tip #9: Develop Unbreakable Patience

Our bodies break down, adapt, and grow. It's a progressive process, and it takes time. If you run too hard too soon, you could find yourself in trouble. Not only will you become incredibly sore, but you increase your chance of injury. Rushing can lead to injury and injury can lead to giving up on your training.

The key to endurance is patience. Our bodies need time to rebuild and grow. If you RUN RUN RUN then you will only STRESS STRESS STRESS. There is no room to heal and grow. Training for a marathon takes patience. Recovering from a run takes patience. Running a marathon takes patience. A marathon mindset is a patient mindset. So have patience in the process and faith in your abilities. Take it one day at a time and the finish line will come.

Marathon Mindset Tip #10: Train With Affirmations

Similar to how your external world is the exact reflection of your internal world, crossing the finish line will come down to your training efforts. Isn't the honesty in running a marathon marvelous? So if you train like a marathon runner, then you will become a marathon runner. It will feel like a natural occurrence. So don't get lost in the smoke. See your reflection in the mirror, and train like you already achieved your goal. Run like you already are a marathon runner.

Here's a trick. Type this affirmation in your phone: "I am so incredibly grateful now that I am a marathon runner." Now save it to your home screen. Read it every time you look at your phone. And since the average person checks their phone between 50-75 times a day, you will really begin to believe you are a marathon runner.

Marathon Mindset Tip #11: Read Until the Impossible Becomes Possible

See the true potential within yourself. Understand the marathon is not an impossibility, but an outcome to a process. Take running a marathon off its pedestal. To do so, read about runners who have accomplished impossible feats. Athletes have run across the United States, down the Appalachian Trail, and across the Sahara Desert.

I've already mentioned how I've run a 200-mile race. One day a marathon seemed impossible, and then… I ran eight marathons in a row during one race. And I don't say that to impress you. I say that to press UPON you that YES, it's possible, and YES, you can do it too!

Know that any distance is possible by anyone. Just re-adjust your lens on the impossible, and suddenly, your possibilities are infinite.

Marathon Mindset Tip #12: Grow at the Speed of Life

When I first heard the saying: "Life is a beautiful struggle," I couldn't help but connect with it. As an endurance runner, you naturally adopt a growth mindset. No longer is anything fixed. For example, there is never a "good runner" or a "bad runner." As long as you are putting in the hard work, growth is always occurring.

The fact is we are either progressing or regressing in everything we do. Nothing in life is static. We are either living or dying, losing weight or gaining weight, becoming stronger or weaker. Even the bones in our bodies aren't a fixed structure, they are living tissue. And despite their hard and solid appearance, bones constantly change throughout our lifetime.

And just like weights in a gym, the resistance – or in this case, our struggles – create growth. They break us down, we learn from them, we adapt, and we grow back stronger, so we can handle more stress. So, when training for a marathon becomes difficult... guess what? It should be! Appreciate the struggle. And as you run through the resistance, it will only increase your endurance. And if you work hard enough, you will develop the endurance to run a marathon.

Make sure to read up on adopting a "growth mindset." When you see the world through GROWTH, everything is either moving forward or moving backward. You begin to see the opportunity in EVERYTHING... even your struggles.

Marathon Mindset Tip #13: Look Past the Heckler

Listen up. You can read a million quotes and consider running a marathon a million times. But without the final step... the ACTION step... your dream of becoming a marathon runner will die in your mind. Understand that thoughts are real things. Your car, your phone, your TV. Even the satellites orbiting the earth... all once were thoughts in someone's mind. And those thoughts would have stayed thoughts if it wasn't for action. It was the ACTION that brought them to life.

Here's a scary thought...

Think of all the potential Michael Jordans who have died through your lifetime. The people who never leveraged their talents. Who went through life without expressing themselves. Who held other people's opinions of themselves higher than their own. Those scared to take a chance, to do what was right in their heart, to follow their dreams. Think of all those people who went through life safe. Who were afraid and didn't dare to move forward on their aspirations. But hey… at least they were liked by others who didn't dream… right?

While training for a marathon, you are going to fall down. Things won't go in your favor. Some days will be exhausting. But for every time you fall down, there's ALWAYS an opportunity to get back up. If one approach doesn't work, then try another. And if that approach doesn't work, then try another. And if the next approach doesn't work, then try another…

No… someone else's opinion of you DOES NOT have to dictate the course of your life…and YES, you can always find a way. Do you want someone to believe in you? Well, I DO.

NO, it won't be easy. But YES, it will be worth it. So look past the heckler in your mind, and the hecklers out of your mind. Listen to your heart. And if something is telling you to run a marathon…then get out the door and start training. There's no better time than RIGHT NOW. To help, tell your mind: "I OWN YOU!" Drop this book RIGHT NOW and go run your first training run. Break up the pattern. You cannot overcome self-doubt from the couch, you need to stand up and take ACTION.

Marathon Mindset Tip #14: Write Your New Story

Some look at running a marathon as a way to better their running. And you may be one of those runners. But the truth is finishing a marathon will do so much more. Yes, it will better your running. But you know what? It will also better your life.

You see, we get stuck telling ourselves the same stories over and over again about who we are. Because that's who we are supposed to be… right? As I mentioned earlier in the book, if you want to change your life, then you must change your story. And becoming a marathon runner will do that to a person. Crossing the finish line is not your happy ending, it's your magnificent beginning… so get out the door and start writing your new story TODAY.

To help, literally sit down and write a new story for your life and read it regularly. Make sure you add being an excellent marathon runner! Want to run Boston? Write it. Want to run multiple marathons per year? Write it. Want to run a marathon on the Great Wall of China? Write it. Whatever you desire most, write it. Write a few paragraphs, read it daily, and watch your story come alive.

Marathon Mindset Tip #15: Expect to Cross the Finish Line

Remember when I said whatever we focus on magnifies in our subconscious mind? That means the seeds you plant today are the trees that grow tomorrow with delicious fruits. Yes, weeds – meaning negative thoughts – will also grow. So get rid of them. Because we all know what happens if you don't get rid of one weed… MORE WEEDS GROW!

Watch what you think, and turn negative thoughts into positive ones. That's the difference of having no drive to train and running out the door with excitement.

Here's a powerful exercise: do not HOPE to run a marathon, EXPECT it. Try it… close your eyes and HOPE to run a marathon. How did you feel? Okay, now… close your eyes and EXPECT to run a marathon. Feel the difference?

Marathon Mindset Tip #16: Take Action NOW

Remember this: KNOWLEDGE is not power… knowledge with ACTION is power. When you read something and then apply it to your life, that's when you improve your running, that's when you improve your life. Again… wouldn't right NOW be a good time to start training? Don't just read these tips or just review *The BASIC Marathon Guide Training Program*. Do your reading, but most importantly, TAKE ACTION.

Marathon Mindset Tip #17: Make a Clear Decision

Do you know when running a marathon really begins? No, it does not begin at the beginning of the race, not in the week building up to it, and not even at the start of your first training run.

So when does running a marathon actually begin? Running a marathon begins when you make a DECISION. And in that decision is where your future is mapped. And when I say a decision, I mean a real, SOLID decision. No "what ifs," no partial commitments, no one foot in and one foot out. I'm talking about a clear and decisive decision to run a marathon.

If you've already made that decision, then guess what? Your training has already begun. Remember this: partial commitments destroy more marathon goals than injuries ever will. So make a clear decision and don't give yourself a way out.

Make a decision RIGHT NOW that you will run a marathon. That's it. No doubts. Hang your training program on your wall and get started.

Marathon Mindset Tip #18: Make Reliability a Priority

As I mentioned, the marathon was the first race I ever ran. It took a leap of faith. After training was complete, I stashed a handful of gels in my pocket, walked the starting line, and thought, "If these thousands of people can run a marathon then why not me?"

So why not YOU?

Believe that's it's possible. Even if you only run up to the point where you must walk to the finish. Do whatever it takes to get the first one done. Reliability will make you feel much more confident. Racing close to home provides reliability. Taking small progressive steps creates reliability. Running with quality gear provides reliability. Be prudent and do whatever is required to instill reliability in your training.

REMEMBER: make sure you get fitted for running shoes that compliment your footstrike. They should also be supportive and comfortable. The right shoe will significantly decrease your chances of injury. When you have a RELIABLE shoe, you will feel a BIG difference when you train. This will help you to believe in yourself more.

Marathon Mindset Tip #19: Frame Hills in a Positive Way

Make your attitude towards hills positive. Don't label them as "tough" or "annoying." The key is to frame them in a positive way.

Here's a trick: focus on your form instead of speed. Keep your strides short, engage the core, pump your arms, and run through the top. Don't be afraid to reduce your effort. You have plenty of time to make up speed on the downhill. When running downhill, look up with confidence. Don't be afraid to let go and let gravity work its magic. Running descents should feel more like a flow than a forced effort.

But whatever you do, frame hills in a positive way. Do this and you will have made a significant step in developing a marathon mindset.

Marathon Mindset Tip #20: Have Zero Tolerance for Excuses

Remember what I said about excuses earlier? I mentioned how we naturally develop them during training. Sometimes to the point of stopping us from even getting to the starting line. If you look for an excuse, it's always there.

You can find excuses in every situation, not just during marathon training. And just like complaining… they are addictive. And you can't eliminate excuses in your running alone. It's about kicking the habit as a whole. So, you must practice eliminating excuses in every aspect of your life.

Here's a trick: go through your entire day without complaining or making a single excuse. If you catch yourself making an excuse, quickly correct it with an empowering thought. Your external circumstances do not create your life, YOU do. If you resonate with this, then you will undoubtedly get through training.

Marathon Mindset Tip #21: Redefine What Competition Means

As a runner with a marathon mindset, you understand that the real race is against yourself. Even during a competition, you are competing against yourself. Just take a look at the definition of "compete." It's not "to brutally beat your opponent to a pulp." Remember, life's not about ME, it's about WE. "Compete" actually means "to strive for an objective." And if you dig deeper, you will find its true meaning. The word "compete" comes from the Latin word *"competere"* meaning to "strive together." So, when we compete, we strive together to reach an objective or goal. Changes your perspective on racing, doesn't it?

Even if you did consider competing on race day, the focus is still from within, not from without. Because in all situations, the real race is against yourself – it always is, and it always has been. So, on race day, don't race against the person next to you. Focus on you and run at a steady pace. Trying to keep up with someone will only drain your energy required for the later stages of the race. Keep your eyes forward to the finish… not on the person next to you.

Marathon Mindset Tip #22: Focus on the Outcome, Not Fear

There are millions of finish lines in the world, but only ONE journey. That is, you only pave one path. YOUR PATH. So enjoy your journey… the one that has no end.

To help, focus on where you're headed rather than what you fear. In other words, focus on the finish line of the marathon, not on the many training days along the way. Don't focus on the details, focus on that triumphant moment of becoming a marathon runner. Everyone's path to becoming a marathon runner is different. We all live different lives, have different body types, and hold different beliefs. But if you focus on the outcome, rather than the "what-ifs," suddenly the road less traveled becomes a favorable place to run.

Marathon Mindset Tip #23: Believe in Others

If you TRY, then you have a chance at finishing a marathon. But if you DON'T TRY, then you have NO chance at finishing a marathon. Don't let negative emotions like fear, disappointment, or regret stop you. Without risk, there is NO celebration. You will have to risk feeling negative emotions to obtain positive ones. Yes, you must take a chance on yourself to finish a marathon. But if you ask me, a chance on yourself is the best bet that life has to offer.

To grow confident in wagering on YOU, start to believe in OTHERS. It will come back tenfold because having positive beliefs will develop into your new way of thinking. It will become a new habit.

To start, don't shortchange people for what seems like a "natural talent." Yes, some people are naturally better than others, but to be great at anything takes HARD WORK. Just look at one of the greatest painters in history, Michelangelo. He said, "If people knew how hard I worked to get my mastery, it wouldn't seem so wonderful at all." And this is the guy who painted the ceiling of the Sistine Chapel!

Marathon Mindset Tip #24: Guide Your Emotions Forward

Race day can create enthusiasm, excitement, AND anxiety. But you know what? They are all one and the same. That's because enthusiasm, excitement, and anxiety are all aroused emotions. And by controlling them, you will have an enormous reserve of energy. But if you let them control you, you may go out the gate too fast. Even if it doesn't feel like you're running above pace at the beginning of a race, chances are… you are running too fast. Race day adrenaline also plays a role. But trust me. Eventually, it wears off. And if you're not careful, you could dig yourself into a race day grave.

As a newcomer, being completely worn out at mile 16 with 10 miles to go is a lonely place. So be eager, but control that energy. Don't let it control you. On race day, pay close attention to your pace at the start. Keep your pace slow no matter what your mind tells you. Race day excitement is persuasive. It will make you feel like you can defy the laws of physics. So be careful and take it slow.

Marathon Mindset Tip #25: Set the Stage for an Enjoyable Run

Improve your internal environment when training by enjoying your external environment. To do so, train during your favorite time of year. You will do a lot more running than usual training for your first marathon. So, make sure you enjoy the weather.

Personally, I love the summer. All my longer races tend to fall in the late summer or early fall. This way, I can train all summer in the heat. Something about stepping out of my door early in the morning to run in the warm summer air feels incredible.

That's versus when I trained for a 116-mile race across the state of Florida in the dead of winter. Sure, I love to run, but regular long runs in below-freezing temperatures were tough. Sometimes it was discouraging. It wasn't nearly as enjoyable as running with the warm summer sunrays shining on my face.

The point is to train in the temperatures you like most. This way, you turn the experience into a pleasant one.

Marathon Mindset Tip #26: Search Beyond the Physical

When running a marathon, you will experience both highs and lows. So try to ride the highs a bit longer, and climb out of the lows a bit faster. Here's how: enjoy and appreciate the race. Isn't it fantastic the way your feet move? How running is a natural act of life? Isn't the freedom of running amazing? How you can run anywhere at any time? What a GIFT.

So when your legs tire, dig deeper. Search for something beyond the physical… something beyond yourself. You know what that something is. The answer lies within your heart. Focus on your intuition… the answer is there. Listen closely and fall in love with the journey.

Right now… look up. If you are inside, then look out the window. Do you see the sky? Do you see that beautiful infinite never-ending sky?

Now close your eyes. Guess what? That same infinite space from above has the same infinite depth that's within you. We could call that POTENTIAL, and in that sense, your potential is limitless.

Marathon Mindset Tip #26.2: Embrace Change and Be Humble

If you ask me, running a marathon has little to do with running and a lot to do with altering the entire course of your life. For me, it was a tool for personal development.

Now don't get me wrong, becoming a better runner and improving your physical health come a close second. But the real prize is in the progress. It's in the development. It's in the change.

Challenges you once thought too difficult… suddenly become just another obstacle to overcome. And instead of getting lost in the details of life, you see the bigger picture. And of course, your self-confidence will sore. But you will have to cross the finish line to change your life… so… what are you waiting for? To help in the process, embrace change and be humble.

Final Thoughts on Developing a Marathon Mindset

Although I now run ultramarathons, I always find time to write about marathon running. That's because finishing a marathon was where all my running began. I know how special it can be. That's why I took the time to write this book. Running has changed my life for the better, and I know it can change yours.

Yes, I've run many ultramarathon distances, but it all started with those 26.2 miles. I will be forever grateful for that distance.

Remember – it all starts in the mind. It all starts with replacing those limiting beliefs. See them for what they are – repetitive negative thoughts – and replace them with positive ones.

Don't be a copy of the running world majority. Or of your parents. Or of your friends. Or of society. Be a copy of yourself, of your passion, and of your intuition. Because the truth is anyone can run any distance… it just takes one more step. Always take ONE MORE STEP.

So start implementing the marathon mindset tips you've just read. Pull out the ones that you resonate with most and save them. Stick them on your desk, or on the home screen of your phone, or frame them to a picture on your wall. Post them to your social media pages, or read this chapter daily, or read them before you sleep and when you wake up.

You can change ANYTHING in your life if you change your beliefs. Start believing that today. When you do that, you'll have found the secret to developing a marathon mindset.

CHAPTER 7:

Bring It Home

I remember the first step I took as a new runner and my last step before finishing my first marathon. At the time, it sure seemed like a whole lot of ground to cover. Now, between training and races, I've run over 100 marathon and ultramarathon distances. But it's never been about the race to finish. It's always been about the journey to travel. You will have bad days and good days, slow runs and fast runs, tough races and easy races. But you will only have one journey. Sure, the path may get challenging, but isn't that true for all roads less traveled?

Remember, when you finish a marathon, you enter into the .5% club. Only .5% of the population has finished a marathon. If it were easy, everyone would do it.

Most of the time when you are new to running, somewhere around mile 18 is where the real challenge begins. This is where you may have the pleasure of meeting "the wall." This is where the pain really sets in. Here is when your mind tells you to STOP! "Come on, what's the point?" "Why are you running this thing anyway?" "Who cares if you quit?" "18 miles was a good effort, let's call it a day!"

But know this: the same wall that blocks disappointment is the same wall that blocks your triumph. The same wall the blocks failure is the same wall that blocks your success. And the same wall that blocks regret is the same wall that blocks your dreams.

Luckily, the moment when your legs give up is the EXACT moment when your heart gives more. It tells you to run for something greater, something worth the pain and worth the struggle. It reminds you of those long months, those tiring days, and those weekend sacrifices. It reminds you how bad you want it and how bad you DESERVE it.

Yes, the wall is a tough barrier to break the first time, but it's absolutely doable. If you keep pushing yourself and you break past that wall, then guess what? The dynamics change completely! All of a sudden, as you move forward, you don't just RUN to the finish line, you GRAVITATE towards it! Those last few miles feel like you're flying as the crowd gets larger, and the cheers get louder, and the finish line comes into vision. Then suddenly, all of those questions of "Is it worth it?" and "What's the point?" instantly disintegrate, along with all the other excuses that tried to stop you from reaching this victorious moment.

And then it happens…you cross the finish line, and suddenly, it all makes sense. Suddenly, you come to realize that you didn't just run a marathon to better your running, you ran it to better your life!

And that's what this guide really provides: a TOOL to change your life for the better.

So with that, I want to thank you from the bottom of my heart. I cannot express enough how incredibly grateful I am that you took the time to read this book. Thank you for allowing me to serve you and be your guide in helping you finish your first marathon.

Thank you, and enjoy every minute of your new life as a marathon runner!

Printed in Great Britain
by Amazon

32686041R00058